i

Contents

CHAPTER **1**

BMAT Section I

1.1 Introduction

The BioMedical Admissions Test (BMAT) is designed to test the academic potential of otherwise similarly accomplished candidates. The test assesses generic academic skills, basic scientific knowledge and written communication ability. Section 1 focuses on the generic academic skills to determine problem solving and critical thinking capacity. This part of the test requires candidates to work quickly and proficiently as this section is time pressured.

Timings and Questions

The statistics for this section are as follows:

- 60 minutes
- 32 Questions
- 1 minutes 52 seconds per question

Scoring in Section 1

Every question is worth 1 mark. There is no negative marking so it is important to answer every question. Total marks are then added up and converted into a standardised BMAT score. On average 5.0 is the median score amongst candidates while 6.0 is considered a good score - placing candidates in the top 10-15%.

For example, in 2020, the score conversion was as follows.

Section 1 score conversion

Total mark	BMAT score
0	1
1	1
2	1
3	1
4	1.3
5	1.6
6	1.9
7	2.2
8	2.5
9	2.7
10	2.9
11	3.1
12	3.3
13	3.5
14	3.7
15	3.9
16	4.1
17	4.3
18	4.5
19	4.6
20	4.8
21	5
22	5.2
23	5.4
24	5.7
25	5.9
26	6.2
27	6.5
28	6.8
29	7.3
30	7.9
31	8.8
32	9

The distribution of BMAT scores is released by the test administrators every year in the format of a histogram. The distribution of Section 1 BMAT scores in 2020 is showcased below. Oxford University advise that

"that the typical average applicant should be working towards a 6 (a 7 is still   fairly rare) in sections 1 or 2" whilst Imperial College London maintain a cut-off of 3.5 in Section 1 and Section 2, with the sum score in these two Sections being at least 10.9. UCL advise that the average candidate invited to interview scored 5.7 in 2021. BMAT score requirements change every admission cycle so candidates are advised to research the requirements of desired universities and set a score goal accordingly. As a general rule, higher BMAT scores are correlated with higher acceptance rates. However, there are many parts to a medicine application beyond BMAT score with each university weighting various parts of the application differently. Therefore, scoring lower than desired can be mitigated by strong performance in other areas.

The histogram below can help candidates set a target Section 1 score. The following chapters can help provide the necessary information and tips to help candidates prepare effectively, and work towards achieving this score.

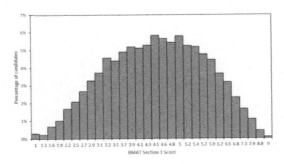

Question Composition

Below is an exploration of the different types of questions found in the BMAT Section 1. Understanding the skills being tested in each question format allows prospective candidates to hone in on these skills in their own practice.

Critical Thinking Questions

In critical thinking questions, a series of logical arguments are presented. Candidates are required to summarise and draw conclusions, identify assumptions, assess the impact of additional evidence, detect reasoning errors, match arguments and apply principles.

Candidates can expect to spend around 30 minutes on critical thinking questions with approximately 16 questions of this type present in the section.

Candidates often find critical thinking questions difficult initially. However, honing in on certain foundational skills, as explored in the following chapters, can significantly improve speed and accuracy, helping increase the score achieved on the day.

Problem Solving Questions

In problem solving questions, candidates are required to efficiently encode and process numerical information to solve problems. They also must be able to recognise the relevant information, discern similar cases and apply the appropriate problem solving strategies where relevant. Typically this involves using simple numerical and algebraic operations to decipher the answer.

This type of question typically takes three formats.

Relevant Section - Candidates are required to filter through large amounts of information quickly and efficiently to identify the relevant details needed to answer the question.

Finding Procedures - Candidates are required to work out the correct mathematical procedure needed to effectively solve a given problem.

Identifying Similarities - These questions require candidates to compare information presented in two different ways, and identify the similarities. Information is typically presented in graphs, tables and charts.

Candidates can expect to spend around 30 minutes on problem solving questions with approximately 16 of these questions present in Section 1. Problem solving questions can often take a long time to work out initially. Thus learning fast ways to approach these questions and honing these skills is essential to improving speed and accuracy and thus, securing a high mark in Section 1 of the BMAT. The following chapters will provide information   and   tips   on   how   to   improve   these   skills.

Scoring Highly on Section 1

Candidates often neglect Section 1 due to an inaccurate perception that Section 1 cannot be prepared for. In order to score highly on Section 1, it is recommended that candidates become familiar with the different types of questions asked. Identifying the different types of questions, and practising them individually, will help improve efficacy on the day. The following chapters provide a breakdown of question types and advice for approaching each individual type of question.

1.2 Conclusions

Conclusions fall within the *Critical Thinking* category of questions. This format will typically present a series of logical arguments and candidates will be required to draw conclusions based on the arguments presented. Although this may sound like an easy task, often, a number of arguments will be presented throughout the passage so identifying the main conclusion can prove difficult. Therefore, practising this type of question is important as it will aid candidates in identifying the key argument.

The Conclusion

A **conclusion** is a single line or phrase that summarises the whole passage. In the BMAT, candidates are asked to either summarise or draw a conclusion. Summarising requires candidates to *identify* the main conclusion based on the arguments provided. Drawing conclusions, on the other hand, requires candidates to *infer* the main conclusion based on the information provided. The following example displays a passage and the corresponding conclusion.

> **Passage:** 'Global temperatures have been rising exponentially over the past 30 years, therefore it is clear that global warming is a real threat.'

> **Conclusion:** 'It is clear global warming is a threat'

Drawing conclusions is an important skill for future medics to have as doctors are often required to draw conclusions about a patient's condition based on all the information provided.

Answering the Question

In order to identify the main conclusion and answer the question correctly, it can be helpful to ask yourself the following five questions.

1. What is the main focus of the argument?

2. What is the author trying to convince me of?

3. If I read this one line would it summarise the whole passage?

4.   Why has this been written?

5.   What is the tone?

These questions will help identify the main conclusion and are explored in depth below.

Cover Test

Before reading the answer options, candidates are advised to read the passage and formulate their own conclusion. Then read the answer options and find the corresponding answer - if there is a corresponding answer then this is a successful cover test and indicates that the candidate has likely found the correct conclusion.

Trigger Words

A number of 'trigger' words can help indicate the main conclusion of the argument including:

- Consequently
- Therefore
- So
- Hence
- Thus
- As
- It is very important
- The most pressing issue
- Most important of all
- It follows that
- This proves that
- The point I'm trying to make is
- The truth of the matter Is
- This shows that
- This indicates that
- To sum up

These words will typically, but not always, precede the main conclusion of the argument. Once the main conclusion has been identified, read the answer options to find the correct answer.

What is the main focus of the argument?

When approaching these questions, it is key to concentrate on the *main* focus of the argument. Have a go at the question below.

Example Question 1

> **Passage:** "It is often suggested that self-esteem is a motivating factor for using social media, and has been described as a "social lubricant". Two scientists investigated Facebook use of 63 students from a Northeastern university and found that participants who updated and viewed their own profiles during their experiment had enhanced self-esteem than those who did not. An explanation for this is that social media offers every user the ability to selectively self-present meaning one is able to display more positively biased aspects about themselves and filter any negative content. It therefore enables users to build an ideal image of themselves online which then boosts their self-esteem - a construct known as identity shift."

Which one of the following best expresses the main conclusion of the above argument?

A - Social media can improve one's self-esteem

B - Social media offers every user the chance to have an alter-ego

C - Social media can make one happier

D - Social media leads to depression

E - Social media is investigated heavily in psychology

Explanation:

What is the main focus of the argument? Asking this question reveals that the main focus of the argument is the causal relationship between social media use and self-esteem. The entire passage focuses on the positive impact of social media on an individual's self-esteem.

Answer: A

What is the author trying to convince the reader of?

This question yields substantial utility when there are multiple arguments presented within the text or when both sides of the argument are discussed. It is important that candidates filter out minor arguments presented on either side of the debate and instead focus on the bigger picture. This will help reveal the author's overarching argument which will often act as the main conclusion.

Example Question 2:

> **Passage:** "The Grenfell Tower fire occurred on 14 June 2017 at the 24 storey Grenfell Tower block of public housing flats in North Kensington, Royal Borough of Kensington and Chelsea, West London. It caused at least 80 deaths and over 70 injuries. The cladding in the building was thought to be one of the reasons the fire spread enormously quickly. The local council opted for a cheaper form which compromised on fire safety and was ultimately a key player in the spread of the fire. If there is not to be a repeat of Grenfell Tower, the government must reconsider its stance on fire safety. The fire is an unfortunate tragedy, as it could have been prevented by rigorous fire tests from governmental policy, dismissed as 'red tape'."

Which one of the following best expresses the main conclusion of the above argument?

> A - The rigorous fire tests are a common example of red tape
>
> B- The Grenfell Tower fire occurred in North Kensington
>
> C - The government must think again about their policies on fires
>
> D - The cladding at Grenfell caused the fire in the building
>
> E - The government is more concerned about costs than safety

Explanation:

What is the author trying to convince me of? In this passage, the author is trying to convince the reader that the current fire safety policies are dangerous and must be reconsidered. The author begins by highlighting the tragic consequences of the current regulations. The author then moves on to explain exactly how the regulations allowed fire safety to be comprised and led to the uncontrollable fire. Before stating that this tragedy could have been avoided by better government policies that mandated more rigorous fire testing. Critically the author states that 'the government must reconsider its stance on fire safety' in order to prevent another devastating fire. Thus the author is trying to convince readers that the current government policies on fire safety need reconsideration.

Answer A is false as we are told that they are dismissed as 'red tape', suggesting it should not be seen as being red tape, although it is and there is no indication that it is 'common'.

Answer B is mentioned in the text but remember we are looking for the main conclusion not one of the conclusions or premises.

Answer D is also true but is not what the passage is getting at.

Answer C is the main conclusion as the author is hinting at the fact that the government can play a role in preventing what happened at Grenfell.

Answer E is something that is slightly opinionated and it could be the case that the government is concerned more about safety than costs, as 'red tape' could be interpreted in many ways. The local council did opt for a cheaper form of cladding, however, it is unfair to extrapolate this to the entire government.

Answer: C

Experts Advice!

Looking for keywords or points mentioned the most number of times can help spot the main conclusion.

If I read this one line, would it summarise the whole passage?

This question is arguably the most helpful to confirm the correct answer has been chosen. If a single line summaries the whole passage then, often it is the main conclusion.

Example Question 3:

> **Passage**: 'If the Moon were in a perfectly circular orbit, a little closer to the Earth, and in the same orbital plane, there would be total solar eclipses every month. However, since the Moon's orbit is tilted at more than 5 degrees to the Earth's orbit around the Sun, its shadow usually misses Earth. The Moon's orbit must cross Earth's ecliptic plane in order for an eclipse (both solar as well as lunar) to occur. The truth of the matter is that solar eclipses are a rare phenomenon and should be appreciated accordingly. In addition, the Moon's actual orbit is elliptical, often taking it far enough away from Earth that its apparent size is not large enough to block the Sun entirely.'

Which of the following could be drawn as a main conclusion from the argument?

> A - The moon's orbit is large enough to block the Sun entirely.
>
> B - The moon's actual orbit is elliptical.
>
> C - Solar eclipses do not happen that often.
>
> D - The moon's orbit is tilted at more than 5 degrees to the Earth's orbit around the Sun
>
> E - The moon is a perfectly circular orbit

Explanation:

If I read this one line, would it summarise the whole passage? Reading the line 'The truth of the matter is that solar eclipses are a rare phenomenon and should be appreciated accordingly.' does indeed summarise the whole passage. It also contains the trigger phrase 'the truth of the matter.' It corresponds with answer C therefore, C is correct. In this example, it can be seen that the whole passage can be summarized by this single line, therefore, this is the conclusion.

Answer: C

Common Trap
The conclusion is not always at the end of the argument, it can be in the middle, beginning or the end.

Why has this passage been written?

Analysing the purpose of the passage, and the intended end goal is important. Focusing on the author's aim through writing the passage can help illuminate the main conclusion, as typically the focus or aim corresponds with the main conclusion.

Example Question 4:

> **Passage:** "Speaking as a scientist, cherry picking evidence is unacceptable. When public figures abuse scientific argument, citing some studies but suppressing others, to justify policies that they want to implement for other reasons, it debases scientific culture. One consequence of this sort of behaviour is that it leads ordinary people not to trust science, at a time when scientific research and progress are more important than ever, given the challenges we face as a human race. The huge increase in the use of private agency staff, for example, inevitably means that money is extracted from the system as profit for the agency, and increases costs for the whole country. We must prevent the establishment of a two-tier service, with the best medicine for the wealthy and an inferior service for the rest. International comparisons indicate that the most efficient way to provide good healthcare is for services to be publicly funded and publicly run. We see that the direction in the UK is towards a US-style insurance system, run by the private companies, and that is because the balance of power right now is with the private companies."

Which one of the following best expresses the main conclusion of the above argument from Professor Stephen Hawking?

A - We should follow the US-style insurance system, run by private companies.

B - There is far too much investment in the NHS

C - The government is not focused on making profit from the

D - There is far too much controversy over the NHS

E - The public should be worried about the future of the NHS.

Explanation:

Why has the passage been written? This is a long passage that contains multiple arguments therefore asking this question helps identify the main conclusion. Looking at the bigger picture, this passage is attempting to draw attention to the current risks facing the NHS including becoming a 'two-tier service' and 'a US-style insurance system'. Overall, the passage is relatively negative and critical about how the NHS is run and it is, therefore, clear that Professor Hawking is unhappy with how it is being run.

Answer: E

Common Trap
A passage can have several conclusions. Ensure you find the main conclusion - the central focus of the argument.

What is the tone? Is the author angry, Happy, disappointed?

The tone of the author's writing can help shed light on the main conclusion. For example, if the tone is happy and optimistic this may suggest that the author agrees with the evidence provided, thus lending the conclusion that the author likely agrees with the main focus. On the other hand, if the author maintains a sceptical and negative tone this may suggest that they are not convinced of the evidence.

Example Question 5:

Passage: "There's an uninterrupted view of the city's dramatic sprawl of poverty from the road bridges that carry daily commuters between the islands and the mainland. Fishing and sand- dredging boats drift to work, heading deep into the lagoon. Many of the slums' wooden huts are on stilts, others are just basic shacks shoddily built on the unstable ground of trodden-down   rubbish   dumps.

Most important of all, nobody knows exactly how many people live in Lagos, but they all agree on one thing; Nigeria's biggest city is growing at a terrifying rate. The UN says 14 million.

The Lagos State government thinks it's nearer 21 million, as rural Nigerians are drawn by the hope of a better life to one of Africa's few mega-cities. By 2050 Nigeria will have twice the population it has today, more than half will live in cities, and about 60% of them will be under 21."

Which one of the following best expresses the main conclusion of the above passage?

A - Lagos' population is growing exponentially

B - Lagos is located in Nigeria

C - The population of Lagos is between 14 million to 21 million

D - There is a great deal of poverty in Lagos

E - The population of Lagos is very young

Explanation:

Answer B - This is true but is not the main conclusion from above.

Answer C - We cannot know this for sure, we just know that the population is estimated differently by two different sources.

Answer D - This is again true but it is not the main conclusion of the argument above.

Answer E - We are told it will be very young by 2050 but not that it is young currently.

Pay attention to: "Most important of all, nobody knows exactly how many people live in Lagos, but they all agree on one thing; Nigeria's biggest city is growing at a **terrifying** rate."

What is the tone? The word 'terrifying' sets a tone of concern and accentuates that Lagos is growing very quickly. Additionally, the trigger words 'most important of all' also draw attention to this sentence.

Answer: A

Experts Advice!

Look for emotive words like 'terrifying' or 'shameful' in the passage as this can give insight into the tone of the writing

Choosing the answer

These five questions should help candidates to determine the correct answer to the question. However, if in doubt, it is recommended that candidates narrow down their choices by eliminating incorrect answers and then make an educated guess based on the remaining options. Practising this skill will help candidates improve in this component of the exam, thereby improving their final score.

Take-home points

1. **What is a conclusion?** A conclusion is a single line or phrase that summarises the whole passage
2. **Spotting Triggers.** Look out for trigger words that signal the conclusion.
3. **The BMAT CT "Cover Test"** Read the passage and decide on its conclusion *before* reading the answer options.

1.3 Assumptions

Assumptions fall under the *Critical Thinking* category of questions. This format will present a series of logical arguments and candidates will be required to identify the assumption made. Unaddressed assumptions in medicine can lead to insufficient investigation and obstruct efficient diagnosis. Therefore, the ability to identify assumptions and critically evaluate arguments is an important skill for future medics to have.

What is an assumption?

An **assumption** is an unexamined belief and unstated reason used to support the conclusion of an argument. Therefore an assumption is a statement that is taken at face value to be correct or definitive without any evidence to support it. Within the BMAT, the assumption cannot be stated within the passage and must hold true for the conclusion to be reached. Thus the aim is to identify a belief that is vital to the argument but unstated within the passage.

The assumption must

1.   Be vital to the argument and conclusion.
2.   Not be stated or evidenced within the passage.

The golden rule of assumptions states that:

Premise + Assumption = Conclusion

For example:

> **Passage:** "Manchester United has invested a significant amount of money in the transfer market. They now have a good chance of winning the Premier League this season."

> **Assumption:** "Investing in the transfer market leads to a higher chance of winning the Premier League."

Example Question 1:

Passage: "In the United States, cigarette smoking is responsible for an astonishing 480,000 deaths per year. In addition to this, 90% of lung cancer deaths are related to cigarette smoking. The increasing publicity of these stats in recent years has led to an apparent shift. We have seen the number of cigarette smokers in recent years falling. Less and less people are deciding to take up this once fashionable pass time."

Which of the following is an underlying assumption?

A - Cigarette smoking damages the Alveoli of the lungs

B - The health damage from cigarette smoking can't be reversed

C - People are keen to avoid health problems associated with smoking

D - People are keen to avoid health problems associated with smoking

E - The majority of people who get lung cancer can cite cigarette smoking as a cause.

Explanation:

In line with the Golden Rule of Assumptions, candidates must deduce the premises and conclusion. In this example, the premises are firstly, that smoking leads to health problems and secondly, that people are becoming more aware of the health problems from smoking. The passage then goes on to conclude that less people are smoking.

Therefore, to spot the assumption it is important to identify the information that bridges the premises and conclusion. Why does an increased knowledge of the health risks of smoking lead to less people smoking? Assumption: People are keen to avoid the health problems associated with smoking.

Here it can be seen that the Premise + Assumption = Conclusion

Answer: C

How to spot an assumption

Candidates are encouraged to ask the two following questions to aid in spotting an assumption.

1.   What needs to be true for this argument to hold?

2.   What external knowledge am I using to draw this conclusion?

Example Question 2:

Passage: England cricket's Alastair Cook has been rated as the best England batsman to ever play the game. He was once captain of the side, but is enjoying the best form of his career now that he is no longer captain of the side. Analysts of the game use number of career runs scored as an indicator of how successful the career of any batsman in the game has been.

Which of the following is an underlying assumption?

A - Alastair Cook has more runs than any other English

batsman.

B - Alastair Cook is no longer captain of the England team

C - Alastair Cook disliked being the England Captain

D - Alastair Cook is a successful batsman

Explanations:

Options B and D can be ruled out as they are explicitly stated in the passage. Let us consider option C. The passage says that Alastair Cook is playing very well now that he is no longer captain. However, this does not mean he disliked being England captain and so we cannot assume this. A drop in form does not mean that he did not like being captain, and the drop in form may not have been a result of the captaincy pressures. This leaves us with option A as the correct answer. It is correct because Alastair Cook is rated as the best England batsman, and the rating of a batsman is done with regards to 'number of career runs.' Therefore we can assume Alastair Cook has more runs than any other batsman.

Answer: A

Expert's Advice!

Common Sense is Key! Sometimes, you have to strip an argument down to its basics and take away any external knowledge. External knowledge of a passage can confuse candidates and cause them to infer information that is not directly supported by the passage. Always pick the answer most supported by the information provided.

The Negative Test

Employing the negative test can help candidates confirm that they have selected the correct answer. To perform the negative test candidates must choose an answer option and place "it is not true that" in front of it. Negating the potential assumption reveals whether this damages the argument or overall conclusion. If it does damage the argument then it can be deduced that this assumption is vital to support the argument. Therefore, performing the negative test can help confirm the correct assumption. Below is a sample to help demonstrate the use and impact of the negative test.

> Passage: Learning a foreign language helps people improve their social skills so we should learn them.

> Answer Options:

> 1. Improving social skills is desirable

> 2. We should try to study all subjects that improve our social skills

When applying the negative test to the aforementioned options, we glean the following information.

Learning a foreign language helps people improve their social skills. Improving social skills is not desirable. But we should learn foreign languages.

This seriously damages the argument as why would an individual learn a foreign language that improves social skills if social skills are not desirable? Therefore this is the correct assumption.

Learning a foreign language helps people improve their social skills. We **don't** have to try and learn all subjects that improve our social skills. But we should learn foreign languages.

Similarly, this negative test does not damage the conclusion as a foreign language is one subject, not all subjects. Therefore, this is not the correct assumption.

Example Question 3:

Passage: "Research has shown that children who are the older siblings tend to earn much more than children who are the younger siblings. It is believed that it is unlikely to do with older siblings being more intelligent. Rather, it is believed to be more likely that to be an older sibling it requires a greater deal of independence and since higher paid jobs, such as investment banking and architecture, require independence skills, it is likely that they will enter these professions. This research did not measure whether the relationship between being the older sibling and earning more was dependent on their IQ. Younger siblings who had a career in show-business and journalism were in the top 10% of earners in the United Kingdom. This suggests that skills such as being independent exist at a greater proportion for older siblings than younger siblings."

Which of the following is an assumption underlying the above argument?

A - Being independent is not essential for a career in medicine or architecture.

B - Younger siblings are guaranteed to secure a job in professions involving show business and journalism.

C - Younger siblings who have a career in show-business and journalism are unlikely to be intelligent.

D - A high level of independent skills is not required for a job such as a news reporter or a celebrity.

Explanation:

Immediately answers B and C can be ruled out as they are not in the question. Next, we use the negative test.

> A: Being independent **is** essential for a career in medicine or architecture.

Older siblings tend to earn much more than children who are the younger siblings. Higher paid jobs such as investment banking and architecture require independence skills, it is likely that they will enter these professions. Being independent is essential for a career in medicine or architecture. This still makes sense therefore A is not an assumption.

> D: A high level of independent skills **is** required for a job such as a news reporter or a celebrity.

Older siblings tend to earn much more than children who are the younger siblings. To be an older sibling requires a greater deal of independence. A high level of independent skills is required for a job such as a news reporter or a celebrity. Younger siblings who had a career in show business and journalism were in the top 10% of earners in the United Kingdom. This does not make sense, therefore D is an assumption.

Answer: D

Expert's Advice!

Elimination is key! Ruling out answers that are obviously wrong first will allow more time to investigate the remaining answer options. This will save valuable time by helping you find the correct answer more quickly.

Example Question 4:

> **Passage:** "Johann, the successful city banker, has grown accustomed to long working days and an overall hectic and stressful lifestyle. An urgent client meeting is happening in his office tomorrow, which means his manager has requested Johann to arrive into the office by 7am. On hearing this news, Johann decided that he will wake up an hour earlier tomorrow morning."

Which of the following is an underlying assumption?

    A - Johann enjoys working for his manager.

    B - Johann exhibits high levels of stress.

    C - Johann usually arrives into the office at 8am.

    D - Johann usually arrives into the office at 6am.

Explanation:

Firstly, identify the conclusion of the passage, which is Johann must wake up an hour earlier tomorrow. The reason for this is that he has been requested to arrive at the office by 7am. We are not told the link between Johann deciding to wake up an hour earlier, and the instructions from his boss. We can only assume that the 7am arrival is an hour earlier than what he is accustomed to. Therefore C is the correct answer. Option A is incorrect as Johann could follow his manager's instructions begrudgingly, option B is incorrect as Johann's stress is explicitly stated in the passage, and option D is ruled out by following the aforementioned analysis that leads us to select option C.

Answer: C

Take-home points

1.   **What an Assumption is.** An assumption is an unexamined belief and unstated reason used to support the conclusion of an argument.

2.   **How to spot an assumption.** An assumption can be found by deducing the unstated information that is vital to the argument.

3.   **Use the negative test.** Placing 'it is not true that' in front of an answer helps candidates identify the correct assumption.

1.4 Flaws

Flaws fall under the *Critical Thinking* category of questions. This type of question will present a series of logical arguments and candidates will be required to identify the flaw in the argument. This type of question tends to be slightly easier than the other critical thinking questions as the flaw is often easier to spot.

What is a flaw?

A **flaw** is something that is questionable and is a reason that the argument would fall apart. Therefore, candidates are looking for a statement that is taken at face value to be correct, or definitive to occur, without any evidence. In order to spot this, when reading the passage it is important to consider the information or approach that prevents an argument from making sense. Often, the flaw is also an assumption. To aid students in identifying flaws in BMAT Section 1 passages, we have further explored the ten most commonly encountered types in the exam.

Ten Types of Flaws

1. The Straw Man

This type of flaw misrepresents or distorts an opposing view, with the purpose of dismissing it. This is achieved by exaggerating, fabricating or misrepresenting a person's argument. The aim of this approach is to present the opposing argument as less reasonable so that the argument given by the author appears more reasonable.

> **Passage:** The school won't let us have a BMAT course without any teacher supervising. They're useless. They just don't want us to do well in the BMAT. We should write a petition.

This passage demonstrates the Straw Man approach as the school's reasons for not allowing the BMAT course are being misrepresented to make it easier to dismiss them. Not enabling the course without any teacher supervision is to do with safeguarding, and is a valid reason for a course not to take place, which is very different from being "useless".

Example Question 1:

Passage: Donald Trump was inaugurated as the 45th President of The United States and one of his main policies was to withdraw from the Paris treaty to stop Global Warming. We are told a lot about how successful Donald Trump is as a businessman and that he therefore is able to make logical decisions and a good president. However I do not see how someone who doesn't care about the environment can be President of the United States.

Which of the following is a flaw in this argument?

A - The argument in believing Trump would make a good President is being misinterpreted as also being against climate change

B - Trump's decision to leave the Paris treaty is being misrepresented as him not caring for the environment.

C- They are attacking the people who believe that Donald Trump is a good president.

D - They are narrowing the options available for the reader

E - The argument represents a slippery slope where one action leads to a chain of reactions.

Answer: B

2. Ad Hominem

This flaw involves attacking the person presenting the argument rather than the actual reasoning behind the given argument. This gives readers a negative view of the source of the other argument, thereby weakening it.

Passage: The government tells us that Brexit is going to be a success and that we will come out of it strongly, but how can we trust them, they don't pay taxes.

In this example, the government are being attacked but the arguments relating to the success of Brexit remain unaddressed. Instead, the focus of the attack is the source of the opinion, here, the government.

Example Question 2:

Passage: Andrew Sanders argues that men and women are paid equally in the BBC and that they care significantly about gender equality. Andrew Sanders would say that because he is male and one of the highest earners at the BBC. It can therefore be assumed that the BBC does not in fact care about equal pay.

Which of the following is a flaw in this argument?

A - The argument rejects the view that the BBC does not care about equal pay based on a remark about the person advancing the view.

B - It is a hasty generalisation

C - It is based on a lack of evidence

D - It believes that a link between two variables is necessarily causal

E - Andrew Sanders works for the BBC and therefore it is biased

Answer: A

3. Slippery Slope

The slippery slope flaw is premised on the assumption that if 'X' happens then 'Y' will happen and consequently, 'Z' will happen, therefore we should not let 'X' happen. This argument is flawed as it does not address the initial event. Additionally, this argument is often flawed because the stated series of events does not necessarily follow logically and lead to the stipulated consequence. There is often no guarantee that 'X' will lead to 'Y' and then 'Z'.

Passage: If we give more people places at medical school then it will mean that more people will apply and more people applying will mean that the application process will be easier and so will attract complacent applicants which will then make complacent medical students and complacent doctors.

Giving more people places at medical school is unlikely to lead to negative consequences. The chain of events that is predicted is illogical and extreme.

Example Question 3:

> Passage: The government should not make it illegal to buy cigarettes. Otherwise the government should also ban alcohol. This would mean junk food and foods high in fat content would also have to be regulated. We will then be forced to brush our teeth every day and exercise more than we can.

Which of the following is a flaw in this argument?

> A- It is suggesting that a minor action will lead to major and ludicrous consequences.
>
> B - Multiple concepts are being brought together and are thought to be the same thing.
>
> C - It is based on an assumption with a lack of evidence.
>
> D - Brushing teeth and exercising more have positive health benefits.

Answer: A

4. Tu Quoque

This type of flaw occurs when an attempt is made to justify an action on the basis that someone else is doing it; it is colloquially thought of as the classic "if they're doing it, why can't we".

> **Passage:** The United Kingdom should leave Paris Agreement that aims to tackle Climate Change because Donald Trump decided to and he is President of the United States

In this case, it is not possible to justify leaving the Paris Agreement on the basis that another country has done it. It can be argued that it was illogical to do so and so another country's views may not necessarily reflect   the   UK's.

Example Question 4:

Passage: "Manchester United have hit their fans with a 12.3% average rise in season ticket prices for the next campaign. A top-price ticket will cost £38 and the cheapest £23... But United have defended the price rises, saying they compare favourably with the rest of the Premiership. 'We do not know what most of our rivals will charge next year, but even a price freeze across the rest of the Premiership would mean that next year only seven clubs will have a cheaper ticket than £23 and nine clubs will have a top price over £38 – in some cases almost double,' said Humby [Manchester United finance director]."

Source: http://news.bbc.co.uk/sport1/hi/football/teams/m/

man_utd/4895330.stm

Which of the following is a flaw in this argument?

A - It makes an assumption that they are not being unfair

B - They are drawing a conclusion that they are being unfairly targeted based on a lack of evidence

C - They are attacking the person disagreeing with the price rises

D - It is possible that all clubs, including Manchester United overcharge, for their tickets.

E - They are comparing a season ticket price in Football to the price of other sports

Answer: D

5. Generalisation

This type of flaw occurs when a statement attributes some characteristic to all, most, or some members of a given set. It is when one says something is true all of the time, for example, when it is only the case some of the time.

Passage: We were having a discussion today at school, and we all have been using Instagram more than Snapchat and so Instagram is now the more popular social media.

There is not a large enough or representative sample size to ascertain whether this is the case. Whilst it may be true, a larger sample size may have revealed something different.

Example Question 5:

Passage: It can be said that biologically, women are weaker. Due to the lack of testosterone in women, they are unable to undertake more of the strenuous jobs, such as heavy lifting. This imbalance of physical attributes is shown when in almost all of the sports worldwide, men and women compete in separate competitions.

Which of the following is a flaw of the argument above?

A - Just because 'X' is 'Y' it does not mean 'B' is 'A'.

B - It is ignoring the fact that there is a lot of bias against females in sport

C - Sport doesn't fully represent the biological status/strength of the genders

D - Testosterone imbalance is not responsible for the differences in physical ability

Answer: C

6. Conflation

This flaw occurs when two statements share some characteristics with one another. Therefore, they are assumed to be a single identity, and the differences between these statements appear to become lost.

Passage: 400 people got 70% average or above on the UKCAT but only 200 people got a 70% average for the BMAT, therefore the BMAT is the harder exam.

Candidates are not given any indication of how many people in total took the UKCAT and the same for the BMAT, as there could have been fewer people taking the BMAT and so proportionally may not be the harder exam.

We cannot accept the conclusion presented as it treats the sample size as the same.

Example Question 6:

> **Passage:** There has been far too much discussion about the risks of binge drinking among under 21's. People are not listening to the facts. The number of deaths caused by binge drinking since 2009 adds up to a total of 37 however the number of deaths caused by taking selfies adds up to a total of 66. The amount of money invested in preventing binge drinking therefore has been a waste, as the comparison with taking selfies clearly shows that binge drinking is not as much of a dangerous risk as many people believe it to be.

Which of the following identify/identifies a weakness in the above argument?

> A -More under 21's will carry out binge drinking if money was not invested in to preventing it.
>
> B - The sample size was too small
>
> C - There may be a smaller number of people who drink than those who take selfies.
>
> D - We aren't given how much money was spent to decide it was a waste.

Answer: C

7. Circular Argument

This flaw occurs when a reason for an argument is the same as the conclusion or you have to assume that the conclusion is correct for the reasons to make sense.

> **Passage:** The bible is the Word of God because God tells us it is in the Bible.

The only reason given for the Bible being the word of God is that it is from the Bible. However, candidates have to assume that the Bible is factual yet it is the very thing being questioned to follow the logic of the argument.

Example Question 7:

Passage: A group of campaigners were campaigning for the protection of animals on behalf of the WWF. They provided proof animals were dying out based on a few statistics they ran in the Amazon rainforest. They argue that endangered species should be protected as it is important to support animals that are threatened.

Which of the following uses the same flawed logic as the argument above?

A - The law should be obeyed because it is the law.

B- Books should not be printed because they cost a lot of

money

C- Coke has sugar and sugar can cause cancer so coke

causes cancer

D- We should use solar panels because we're running out

Answer - A

8. Restricting the Options

This flaw occurs when a small number of choices are presented which helps to support one specific opinion.

Passage: Either we keep the risk of innocent school children being murdered in broad daylight or we accept that we need new gun laws.

The only reason given for introducing legislation for gun licenses is that it is assumed it is the only possible solution to the risk of the murder of innocent school children and does not consider that there may be many others. It also appeals to the reader's emotions.

An Example Question 8:

Passage: Either a creator brought the universe into existence, or the universe came into existence out of nothing. The universe didn't come into existence out of nothing as nothing comes from nothing. This means that a creator brought the universe   into   existence.

Which of the following uses the same flawed logic as the argument above?

> A -Every person who votes in the election votes for either Labour or Conservative

> B - A legal case settled by Mike Ross is invalid because Mike Ross is a fraudulent lawyer.

> C- Lincoln Burrows was put in jail and therefore he is a criminal

> D - If you fail the BMAT, you won't make a good doctor

Answer: A

9. Causation vs Correlation

This flaw occurs when 'X' and 'Y' have both changed in a certain way, but could be completely unrelated. Just because 'B' follows a pattern with 'A', we should not wrongly assume that 'B' has caused 'A'.

> Passage: Over time, the number of people smoking has risen as well as the number of people with cancer. Cancer therefore is caused by smoking.

This does not consider the fact that there may be other factors which are causing cancer, and while there is a correlation between the two variables this could just be down to chance and is not necessarily causal.

Example Question 9:

> **Passage**: Homeless population and crime rate might be correlated, in that both tend to be high or low in the same locations. It is equally valid to say that homeless population is correlated with crime rate, or crime rate is correlated with homeless population. To say that crime causes homelessness, or homeless populations cause crime are different statements.

Why is the above statement true?

> A   -   It   is   making   a   large   generalisation

B - It is restricting the options

C - It is a circular argument

D - Correlation does not mean causation

Answer: D

10. Syllogism Flaws

This type of flaw occurs when a relationship exists between two variables in one direction. Therefore, it is assumed that it is also true for the two variables in the opposite direction or a third or fourth variable.

Passage: Some of A are B and some of B are C. Therefore some of A are C.

There could be some B that are A but are not C. We need to question whether it is the same units of B that are A are also the same units that are C.

Example Question 10:

Passage: All spoons are cherries. Some cherries are apples. All spoons are apples.

Which of the following conclusions are false?

A - Some spoons are cherries

B - All cherries are spoons

C - Some spoons are apples

D - Some cherries are not apples

Answer: B

Take-home points

1. **What is a flaw?** Something that stops the argument from making sense.

2. **10 types of flaws.** Practice spotting these common flaws

3. **Worked   Examples:**   Practice   makes   perfect!

1.5 Effect of Evidence

Effect of Evidence questions fall under the *Critical Thinking* section of the exam. In this component of the test, candidates will be presented with a series of logical arguments and will be required to assess whether the information provided strengthens or weakens the given argument.

What are effect of evidence questions?

Effect of Evidence questions assess how well candidates are able to judge whether the information presented weakens or strengthens an argument that is being made. This is an important skill for future medics as doctors are often required to sift through investigation results to determine the extent to which results confirm or rule out a potential diagnosis. Similarly, doctors are required to sift through a patient's history for the same purpose. These questions require candidates to understand what the aim of the passage is and measure the extent to which a piece of evidence helps to add to the case being presented.

Common Trap

Try and find the conclusion first before looking for the effect of evidence.

Candidates are advised to begin by establishing the main argument. Then read the answer options and determine the extent to which they strengthen or weaken the main argument.

"If it were true" test

Candidates are recommended to use the "If it were true test" in order to assess whether an argument strengthens or weakens a theory. For example, Candidates should ask 'if statement 'B' was true, would it strengthen   or   weaken   the   argument?

Example Question 1:

Passage: The Yerkes–Dodson law is the most accurate measure between arousal and performance at work, and was originally developed by renowned psychologists Robert M. Yerkes and John Dillingham Dodson in 1908. The law dictates that performance increases with physiological or mental arousal, but only up to a point. When levels of arousal become too high, performance decreases. The process is very well illustrated graphically as a bell-shaped curve which increases and then decreases with higher levels of arousal. 20 studies have then shown the accuracy of the graph to be profound.

Which of the following, if true, most seriously undermines the argument?

A - These 20 studies took place at one workplace

B - There are alternative measures of arousal and performance

C - The relationship between arousal and performance is constantly investigated

D - The point at which arousal is reached varies depending on the person

E - There are other ways to illustrate the Yerkes-Dodson law

Explanation:

To deduce the answer candidates must first establish the main conclusion and the premises behind it. The conclusion is that The Yerkes-Dodson law is the most accurate measure between arousal and performance. The premises for this are firstly, it is illustrated well graphically and secondly, 20 studies have shown the accuracy of the graph. Candidates are advised first to rule out answers that are incorrect using common sense, for example, candidates should rule out any answers that do not relate to undermining   the   argument.

Following this, candidates should invoke the 'if it were true that' test on the remaining options.

Thus, Answer B can be ruled out as the fact that there are alternative ways to measure arousal and performance doesn't affect the fact that Yerkes-Dodson may be the most accurate.

Answer C can be ruled out as the fact that it is constantly investigated does not weaken the argument of it being the most accurate measure.

Answer D can be ruled out as the point at which people reach arousal does not affect whether the test is the most accurate.

Answer E can be ruled out as the fact that there are other ways to illustrate the Yerkes-Dodson law that does not influence the argument.

Therefore, A is the correct answer. This shows that sometimes just using logical reasoning can help us reach the correct answer.

Answer: A

Example Question 2:

> **Passage**: The series of protests and demonstrations across the Middle East and North Africa that commenced in 2010, became known as the "Arab Spring", and sometimes as the "Arab Spring and Winter", "Arab Awakening" or "Arab Uprisings" even though not all the participants in the protests were Arab. The Arab Spring was not a complete success, but overall it was more of a victory than a failure and helped revolutionise countries. The Arab Spring fought, in most cases successfully, against social, economic and political injustices. One example of this was when, Egyptian protesters took to the streets against Hosni Mubarak, whose rule was recognised by police brutality and the suppression and repression of civil and political rights, on January 25th 2011. Three weeks later Mubarak stepped down as President of Egypt.

Which of the following, if true would weaken the argument above?

> A - Egypt is still suffering economic problems to this day.

B - Hosni Mubarak was suffering from health problems which made it difficult for him to carry out his duties prior to his resignation.

C - The Arab Spring was influenced heavily by social media

D - Several civilians were killed in the Arab Spring

E - The Arab Spring is not recognised as a United Nations movement.

Explanation:

This passage draws the conclusion that overall it was more of a victory than a failure and helped revolutionise countries. This is based on the premises that firstly, The Arab Spring fought, in most cases successfully, against social, economic and political injustices and secondly, Mubarak stepped down as President of Egypt.

Statement B does weaken the argument as it suggests that another reason other than the Arab Spring led to Hosni Mubarak stepping down and it was therefore not influential. Statement A does not weaken the argument as the conclusion of the argument does not relate to any economic activity. Statements C, D and E are also irrelevant to the conclusion.

Answer: B

Expert's Advice!

Direct contradictions tend to be the easiest items to spot in terms of weakening arguments.

Example Question 3:

Passage: One of the several advantages citizens from all democratic countries have, is the opportunity to choose their chief in command. As a commonwealth under the United States, Puerto Rican citizens are unfortunately unable to vote during the presidential campaign. They are allowed to participate in presidential primaries but not the final event. This is somewhat of an insult to the younger generation on the island. Some of those being sent off to fight wars representing the U.S. having been denied the privilege to choose the person who   is   sending   them.

As an independent nation Puerto Ricans would have the right to participate in elections choosing who their leader would be therefore Puerto Rico ought to be independent and refuse commonwealth to the United States of America.

Which of the following would weaken the argument above?

A - Puerto Rico depends heavily on the United States of

America for its economy

B - Puerto Rico would not be a democratic state but would

introduce legislation for a dictatorship

C - Puerto Rico has previously been independent from the

USA

D - Puerto Rico relies heavily on its younger generation.

E - Other countries that have become independent have

benefited strongly in terms of their healthcare system.

Explanation:

The conclusion of the passage is that Puerto Rico ought to be independent and refuse commonwealth to the United States of America. This is based on the premise that as an independent nation Puerto Ricans would have the right to participate in elections to choose their leader. Thus, the main argument is that if Puerto Rico became independent, its citizens would have sovereignty over their own decisions, however, if it was a dictatorship then this wouldn't occur therefore B weakens the argument.

Answer: B

Take-home points

1. **Approaching Effect of Evidence Questions**. Begin by establishing the conclusion then look at the answers to determine the correct response.

2. **"If it were true" test.** This test can help candidates effectively decipher the correct answer.

3. **Looking for Direct Contradictions.** Direct Contradictions are the easiest answers to spot; look for an answer option that directly contradicts the main premise or conclusion.

1.6 Matching Arguments

Matching Arguments questions fall under the *Critical Thinking* component of the test. This type of question will present a passage and candidates will be required to draw parallels between the arguments in the question and the answer options.

How to Approach these Questions

Firstly, candidates are advised to scan the passage and get a gist of the logic used. Following this, the goal is to determine the basis of the argument, and the principles that the argument is based on. Finally, students should apply the same logic to one of the answer options to select the correct response.

TIMING TIP!

For matching argument questions, it is best to find the principle and plan of the argument the author has used in the text and then look at the answer options. This ensures that candidates do not get bogged down with the content of the passage, but instead focus on how the author has constructed their argument. After all, this premise should be replicated in the answer options.

Matching the arguments, also known as parallel reasoning, is an important skill for future medics to hone as doctors are often required to spot similarities in cases based off patient information only. The ability to spot patterns in information will be important in a medic's career.

Example Question 1:

> **Passage:** I cannot get any answer when I dial my mother's number. Either she is not answering her phone or she has decided to stay away on holiday for an extra week. She must still be away. She would never let the phone ring without answering   it.

Which of the following most closely parallels the reasoning used in the above argument?

A - If I want to remain fit and healthy, I have to watch my diet and take exercise. I want to stay fit, so I eat carefully and go running regularly.

B - If Denise had carried on going to the gym and eating sensibly, she would never have got so run down. She did get run down, so she must either have given up her diet or stopped going to the gym.

C - Joe is looking a lot fitter. Either he has cut down on his eating or he has been out running every day. I know for a fact that Joe couldn't keep to a diet, so it must be exercise that's done it.

D - Anyone who swims over twenty lengths a day has to be pretty fit. Sheena swims thirty lengths a day. Therefore, Sheena must be quite fit.

E - Sticking to a diet is hard at first but after about two weeks most people get used to it. I have been dieting for nearly two weeks so I should be getting used to it soon.

Explanation:

This question is short and evidently flawed. However, the examiners want to see if candidates are able to apply the same logic used in the passage to select the correct answer option. The pattern of this passage involves the author presenting two potential explanations for why their mother cannot pick up the phone. The author then picks one explanation without any further justification/ reasoning.

Option A: This is not correct as it doesn't follow the pattern used in the passage.

Option B: This is not correct as it doesn't follow the pattern used in the passage.

Option C: In this statement the author has presented us with two options, then without further reasoning/ explanation, the author says that Joe has become fitter because of exercise. This follows the same pattern as the passage, so this is the correct answer option.

Option D: The statement is not logically flawed and doesn't match the pattern in the passage, so it is not correct.

Option E: This is not correct as it doesn't follow the pattern used in the passage.

Answer: C

TIMING TIP!
Eliminate answers that are clearly wrong first. Then investigate the remaining options to see which one follows the pattern of the argument most closely.

Example Question 2:

Passage: How did the Earth get its water? It seems it had it all along. There are two possible sources for our water: either bombardment by meteorites soon after Earth's formation, or it was present in the dust from which our planet formed. So, a team from the University of Glasgow looked at the ratio of heavy hydrogen – an isotope known as deuterium – and normal hydrogen in water trapped for 4.5 billion years in volcanic rock. They found little sign of deuterium, which rules out meteorites since they have much more of this isotope. Instead, the water must have originated in the dust cloud from which the solar system, including Earth, condensed.

Which one of the following most closely matches the reasoning in the above argument?

A -Soil is either acidic or alkaline, but there are camellias growing here, which cannot tolerate alkalinity, so this soil must be acidic.

B - Were the dinosaurs warm-blooded or cold-blooded? Obviously, they were cold-blooded since they were reptiles and all reptiles are.

C - A planet that is neither too hot nor too cold to support life is known as a 'Goldilocks planet'. Since many of these exist in the universe, there must be life on some of them.

D - There are two possible ways to get to the airport; bus or taxi.

A taxi will get you there faster, but since the bus is cheaper, most people travel by bus instead.

Explanation:

The argument in the passage is constructed such that there are two possible variables that could explain how Earth got its water. Firstly, it came from dust which formed the earth *or* secondly, it came from bombardment by meteorites. The passage then rules out the second option as deuterium is heavily present in meteorites, and not much deuterium was found. Therefore, the only plausible source of water on this earth is through the dust that condensed to form earth.

Statement A follows the same reasoning. There are two variables, an outcome and a measure of a variable to prove or disprove one of those variables. The variables are that the soil is *either* acidic *or* alkaline. The outcome is the ability to grow flowers, in this case, it is camellias. Given that camellias cannot tolerate alkaline soil, the soil on which camellias exist must therefore be acidic.

Answer: A

Expert's Advice!

If at first, the answer isn't obvious, try getting rid of answer options that you are sure are incorrect. Look for answers that clearly do not follow a similar pattern of reasoning and rule them out. This can help narrow down options to 2 or 3 answers, even if you have to make an educated guess at this point, statistically you have a higher chance of selecting the right answer due to a smaller pool of options.

These questions can be particularly difficult as candidates are normally expected to analyse the content of the text, but in these questions, they are not supposed to look at the content of the text. Instead, they are to look at the underlying principles behind the construct of the text. Therefore, ruling out obviously incorrect answers can help narrow down the choices, this will help save time, especially when checking back over answers at the end.

Example Question 3:

Passage: If you want to earn a good salary these days, you have to gain considerable experience of working abroad. Since I've always wanted to earn a huge salary, it's obvious that I'm going to have to leave this country for some period of time.

Which of the following most closely parallels the reasoning used in the argument above?

A - If I had more time to spend on this project, I know that it would be very successful. I've been told that I'm not going to be given enough time, so the project isn't going to succeed.

B - Sam knew that if he wanted to write a film script, he'd have to learn the special techniques needed for such scripts. He has enrolled on a course to learn how to write them, so he'll soon be writing his

C - If the Foreign Secretary can bring the two sides together for talks, there's a good chance for peace. Peace is something that both sides want, so he'll be talking to both sides soon.

D - If the doctor thinks that you should be allowed out of bed for a short while, then you must be recovering well from your operation. You have recovered much quicker than she thought you would have, so you'll be out of bed a lot from now on.

E - Annie says that if she really wants to win the London Marathon race, she'll have to train very hard every day. She told me that she is determined to win the London Marathon, so that means she'll be working hard on her training programme every day from now on.

Explanation:

There is a pattern again in the passage. If you want 'X' then you must have 'Y', since the author wants 'X' then they must do 'Y'. In the passage, 'X' is earning a good salary and 'Y' is gaining experience abroad. Answer E follows this logic with 'X' denoting winning the London Marathon and 'Y' is training hard every day.

Answer Option A: The statement doesn't match with the pattern of logic presented in the passage, and so, is incorrect.

Answer Option B: The timing component here means that the statement doesn't match the pattern in the passage, as the author says he will soon be writing his first script. B is therefore incorrect.

Answer Option C: This answer is incorrect as 'X' *may* lead to 'Y' but is not guaranteed. 'X' is the foreign secretary bringing the two sides together for talks and 'Y' is a *chance* for peace. It's not guaranteed therefore, C is incorrect

Answer option D: The statement doesn't match with the pattern of logic presented in the passage, so D is incorrect

Answer option E: This is the correct answer as it follows the same pattern shown in the passage.

Answer: E

Logical Flaws

Sometimes questions will ask candidates which of the given statements commit the same logical flaw as the argument presented in the question. Here, candidates are advised to follow the same principles. Begin by scanning the passage to get the gist, then establish the basis of the argument; in this case, what is the basis of the flaw? Finally, apply the same logic as to why that is the flaw of the argument to the answer options.

Common Trap

Don't be thrown by being asked to apply parallel reasoning in a different way. Use the same approach advised for matching arguments.

The last question was a great example of this. Candidates could easily be thrown by this style of question, as it uses parallel reasoning, flaw recognition and understanding skills. Take it step-by-step, apply the matching argument principles and this will help identify the correct answer.

Take-home points

1. **Read the question line first.** The content does not matter, rather the pattern of logic does.

2. **Find the principle behind how the author has formed their argument.** Look for patterns in reasoning.

3. **Apply this logic to the answer options.** Find the answer the most closely   parallels   the   pattern   of   the   passage.

1.7 Applying Principles

Applying Principles questions fall under the *Critical Thinking* component of the test. This type of question will present a passage and candidates will be required to identify the underlying principle. Following this, the answer option which most closely parallels the underlying principle must be successfully selected.

How to Approach these Questions

Candidates are advised to first read the text and identify the underlying principle of the passage. There are two questions that can help illuminate the underlying principle of the passage.

1. What is the conclusion?
2. What is the reasoning?

This should help clarify the principle of reasoning the argument is reliant on. Following this, the goal is to to read the answers and select the one that best represents the underlying principle.

The skill of identifying similarities in the underlying principle is another form of parallel reasoning. Parallel reasoning was required in the previous chapter *Matching Arguments* and is an important skill for future medics to hone, as doctors are often required to spot similarities in cases based off patient information.

Expert's Advice!

Pay more attention to how the argument is constructed than what the passage says, as this pattern of arguments is what you are looking to replicate in the answer options.

Example Question 1:

Passage: Every motorist pays the same amount for road tax,
regardless of how much they use the roads: someone who
covers as little as 1 000 miles pays the same as someone who
covers 20 000. This is unfair. Road tax should be scrapped and
the money raised by an increase in the tax on car fuel. Making
this change would ensure that those who use the roads more
would pay more. This would not only be a fairer system but
could also bring in more revenue.

Which of the following best illustrates the principle underlying the
argument above?

A- People should receive free medical treatment only if they
cannot afford to pay for it.

B - People who travel to work every day by train should pay a
lower fare than those who travel only occasionally

C - People who earn more than double the average wage C
should be made to pay much higher charges for dental
treatment.

D - Television channels should be paid for by subscription so
that only those people who watch them should be made to
pay.

E - Telephone charges should be higher for business customers
than for domestic customers because they are using the
system only to make money.

Explanation:

The principle of the argument in the passage is that motorists should be
paying fuel tax rather than road tax. This is because the author believes
that if you use the roads more, you should pay more. The author believes
individuals should pay for what they use. D maintains this underlying
principle.

Answer Option A: The underlying principle of this statement does not
match the principle in the passage. Therefore, Option A is incorrect.

Answer Option B: This statement is the opposite of what the author is trying to get across in the passage. Here, the underlying principle is that those who travel more should pay less, and those who travel less should pay more. Therefore, B is incorrect.

Answer Option C: The different components in this argument are not connected; dental treatment is not connected to wage, whereas in the passage the author clearly linked activity to the amount you have to pay to use that activity. Therefore, C is incorrect.

Answer Option D: This statement clearly mirrors the underlying principle in the statement. It's saying those that watch TV, should be the ones who pay for TV. Therefore, D is correct.

Answer Option E: This statement shows a disconnected argument and does not link activity to the amount you have to pay. The underlying principle of this statement does not match the principle in the passage. Therefore, D is incorrect.

Answer: D

The Substitution Test

Candidates are advised to apply the substitution test if they are stuck between two answer options. This involves substituting in the main points from the text to see if it follows the same underlying principles. This simple trick easily identifies the correct answer. This is because correct answers will follow the same principle of the arguments therefore, substituting in the points to the correct answer will sound like the text. It is important to narrow down options before employing this approach as it is time consuming. Cross out answers that are obviously incorrect, then employ this method on the remaining 2 or 3 options.

Example Question 2:

Passage: The treatment of unauthorised immigrants by many countries is often cruel and lacking in compassion. Even refugees from war-torn or famine-stricken regions can find themselves imprisoned on arrival or deported back to the place they have fled. It is a terrible decision to have to take, but if we make an exception to the law for one person, we ought to make the same exception for everyone. If some illegal entrants were allowed to stay, others would have to be treated equally, and no country — especially one that is already overpopulated - could physically accommodate the numbers that would then follow. The regulations have to be enforced rigidly, even if this means turning away people in great need.

Which of the following best illustrates the principle underlying the argument above?

A- People should receive free medical treatment only if they cannot afford to pay for it.

B - Growing urban traffic congestion means that in the future the numbers of cars entering some city centres will have to be restricted.

C- All shoplifters must be prosecuted because if one is let off others would rightly expect the same leniency.

D- There is no one rule that can be applied for all prisoners seeking parole: every case is different and should be decided on its merits

E - If there are not enough hospital places for all those who need them, the most urgent ones must be treated first even if others have waited a long time.

Explanation:

The author in the passage is saying that there must be consistency in the way that illegal entrants' entrance to the country is regulated. C matches this underlying principle.

Answer Option A: This statement differentiates people based on their wage, which goes against the principle in the passage where the author is saying everyone should be treated the same. If the statement did match the passage, it would say that wage doesn't make a difference to medical treatment, so everyone must receive the same medical treatment. Therefore, A is incorrect.

Answer Option B: This statement doesn't contain any principles that the author has threaded into the passage- rather the statement is more factual. Therefore, B is incorrect.

Answer Option C: This statement clearly mirrors the principles laid out in the passage. Therefore, C is correct.

Answer Option D: This statement is opposite to what the author is saying in the passage. It goes against the principle in the passage where the author is saying everyone should be treated the same. Therefore, D is incorrect.

Answer Option E: This statement goes against the author's principle of fairness and consistency for everyone. The statement differentiates patients based on urgency, so it doesn't match the principle laid out in the passage. Therefore, D is incorrect.

Answer: C

Common Trap

Although we are looking for the principle that underpins it, the principle is harder to find if you don't understand the argument to start with. You cannot match up the principle if you do not know what you are looking for.

This costs many candidates valuable time by simply not understanding the argument of the text. Along with this, many candidates don't understand the principles seen in the answers, again through a lack of understanding of the arguments being made. Taking the time to read these carefully will save time on the overall question and increase the chance of getting the correct answer.

Take-home points

1. **Understanding the argument.** Candidates must first read through the text to understand the argument.
2. **Find the principle of the argument.** Candidates must then deduce the principle underlying the argument.
3. **Applying the principle of this argument.** Candidates must then find the answer option that shares this principle.

1.8 Date and Time

Date and Time questions fall under the *Problem Solving* component of the test. This type of question will present a passage with information and candidates will be required to apply the correct procedure to calculate the answer. There is no calculator provided therefore, it is essential to brush up on relevant mental arithmetic skills prior to sitting the test.

Problem Solving in Medicine

Problem solving is an essential skill for future medics to have. Doctors have to use this type of reasoning to deduce what is going on with a patient. The ability to understand and solve a problem is a prerequisite for correctly identifying and diagnosing conditions amongst patients. In particular, date and time calculations will be important for prescribing the correct dosage of medications, calculating the cumulative dose and identifying time scales in a patient history. Therefore, honing these skills is not only good for BMAT scores but also, for your future career.

Key Facts

It is important that candidates memorise the following information for the BMAT. This information is assumed knowledge for the test, meaning that candidates are expected to have a comprehensive understanding of these figures and may be expected to use them in calculations.

- 365 days in a year
- 366 days in a leap year
- 1 day = 24 hours
- 1 day = 1440 minutes
- 1 day = 86400 seconds

Expert's Advice!

If a question asks you to look for the number of weeks in a year, find a difference that is divisible by 7.

Months with 31 Days

- January
- March
- May
- July
- August
- October
- December

Expert's Advice!

If a question asks you to look for months of the year, find a difference that is divisible by 12.

Months with 30 Days

- April
- June
- September
- November

Expert's Advice!

If a question asks you to look for two dates that fall on the same day of the week, the number of weeks between these dates must be a multiple of 7.

The Knuckle Trick

There are a number of tricks which can help candidates memorise which months have 30 days and which months have 31 days. One such trick is the knuckle trick outlined below.

1. Make a fist with either of your hands (this can face away from you or towards you)
2. Tap on each of your knuckles and the wells in between

Your knuckles (higher up than the wells in between) represent the months with 31 days, i.e.; higher up equals a higher number of days. The wells in between represent the months with 30 days, i.e.; lower down equals a reduced number of days. All you really have to remember is that February only has 28 days (or 29 in a leap year).

Example Question 1:

> **Passage:** Four friends, Jack, Ni-Yung, Sophie and Lisa are all guessing each other's birthdays. Their birthdays are on the 114th, 163rd, 172nd and 129th days of the year.

Which two friends have their birthdays on the same day of the week as each other every year?

> A - Jack and Ni-Yung
>
> B - Jack and Sophie
>
> C - Jack and Lisa
>
> D - Ni-Yung and Sophie
>
> E - Ni-Yung and Lisa
>
> F - Sophie and Lisa

Explanation:

First of all, we should establish that there are six different combinations. Each name has been abbreviated to represent a letter. Always write out the information in a concise and more understandable format.

J N S and L represent the four names of each friend.

- J - 114
- N - 163
- S - 172
- L - 129

Then work out the possible combinations. For two dates to be on the same day of the week, they must be a multiple of 7 days apart therefore, we must calculate how many days apart the birthdays are.

J + N	163 - 114	49
J + S	172 - 114	58
J + L	129 - 114	15
N + S	172 - 163	9
N + L	163 - 129	34
S + L	172 - 129	43

Testing the gap between each combination shows only J and N have a multiple of 7 in between them, 49. The correct answer is therefore A, Jack and Ni-Yung.

Answer: A

Common Trap

Be careful with your notations on your paper. It can be easy to make small mistakes in working out, this will result in incorrect calculations. Make sure to check your answers - especially if they do not match an answer option exactly.

Example Question 2:

Passage: Four friends called Max, Mark, Julie and Jennifer are guessing each other's birthdays. They are all born in the same calendar year, on the 21st of each month. Coincidentally, their names begin with the first letter of the month they were born in. They are born in different months. No-one is born in January. Max and Julie's birthdays are four months apart. Mark and Jennifer's birthdays are one months apart.

How far apart are Julie and Mark's birthdays?

A - 1

B - 2

C - 3

D - 4

E – 5

Explanation:

We are told that Max and Julie's birthdays are four months apart. We therefore need to look for an 'M' and 'J' that are four apart. We find that March and July are four months apart; therefore, Max is born in March and Julie in July. We are also told that Mark and Jennifer's birthdays are one month apart. We therefore need to look for an 'M' and 'J' that are one apart. May and June fit this, and so, Mark is born in May, and Jennifer is born in June. We are interested in Julie and Mark's birthdays - Julie - July, Mark - May.

They are two months apart, therefore the correct answer is B, 2.

Answer: B

Expert's Advice!

Whenever you are dealing with months in a year questions, it helps to write them out.

J F M A M J J A S O N D

This makes counting differences easier and reduces the chance of calculation or notation errors.

Example Question 3:

> **Passage:** Mary Berry is baking cookies for her TV show. She makes the cookies in batches of 6, and it takes her 30 minutes to prepare a set of 6 cookies. She then puts them in the oven for 20 minutes and during this time, she can work on the next batch. Once she has finished baking the cookies, she leaves the cookies out for 5 minutes and has to monitor them to see when it has been 5 minutes. She is making 30 cookies.

If she starts at 2pm, what time will she finish?

>   A - 5:15pm
>
>   B - 5:40pm

C - 6:15pm

D - 6:50pm

E - 7:00pm

F - 7:15pm

Explanation:

Firstly, we should recognise how many batches she is cooking. Dividing 30 by 6 gives us 5 batches. To cook the first batch, it will take her 30 minutes to prepare, 20 minutes to cook and 5 minutes to monitor; overall this means the first batch will take 55 minutes. However, during the 20 minutes the first batch is in the oven, she can start work on the 2nd batch, giving her a 20 min head start. Thus, she will only need another 35 minutes for each subsequent batch of cookies as she can always use the 20 minutes while one batch is in the oven to prepare the next batch.

Hence total time taken is;

55 + (35 x 4)

Therefore, it is 195 minutes or 3 hours and 15 minutes. Mary starts at 2pm, and the baking takes 3 hours and 15 minutes, therefore this means the baking ends at 5:15pm.

- Batch 1 will finish at 2:55
- Batch 2 finished at 3:30
- Batch 3 will finish at 4:05
- Batch 4 will finish at 4:40
- Batch 5 will finish at 5:15

Answer: A.

Expert's Advice!

Try to spot ways of answering questions quickly. In the example above calculating the time difference was 35 minutes for reaming 4 batches is considerably quicker than working out the timings for each batch. Ensure to apply the correct mathematical procedure to speed up calculations.

Example Question 4:

Passage: Glynnis received a digital clock for her birthday that shows the date and time. Glynnis observed this on her clock. She noticed that all the numbers on her clock were cube numbers. She realised that this had just occurred twice before in the same hour, and that this was the last time it would occur this year. She will have to wait until January for it to occur again.

In January, how many times will Glynnis' clock display only cube numbers and zeros?

    A - 18

    B - 22

    C - 27

    D - 30

    E - 34

Explanation:

For this question, it would be good to note what cube numbers are.

- Cube Numbers: 1, 8, 27, 64

These are the only cube numbers we need as 01 will be the month, the day can be between 1 and 31, the hour between 1 and 24 and the minute between 1 and 60. looking for cube numbers within these brackets gives us the following options.

- Months: 1
- Days: 1, 8, 27
- Hour: 1, 8
- Minute: 1, 8, 27

For example, in January, there are three days this will occur - 1st, 8th and 27th January.

On the 1st, it will occur at: 01:01, 01:08, 01:27, 08:01, 08:08 and 08:27. It will occur at the same times on the 8th and the 27th as well. It will therefore occur 18 times, so the answer is A, 18.

Answer: A

Common Trap!

Be robust with the set of rules presented. Ensure you do not miss key components of the question by misreading the rules or failing to fully implement them. For example, in the question above make sure to note all the cube numbers. Similarly, make sure to remember January has 31 days.

Example Question 5:

Passage: A nurse is going through some spreadsheets to find the reference number for a baby born in the ward. Each baby is given a 8 digit reference number. Example: 15724425. The baby was the 42nd baby ever born at the clinic, on 24th October 2004. 157 represents 157 months since the first baby in the clinic was born, 24 represents the day the baby was born. The last number represents the last value of what the previous 7 digits add up to i.e. (1 + 5 + 7 + 2 + 4 + 4 + 2 = 25 so 5).

Which one of these is the correct reference number for a baby born on the ward?

A - 19231174

B - 19431468

C - 19531505

D - 19631639

E - 20031234

Explanation:

Firstly, we should split up the six-digit code into a more understandable format.

- A. 192 31 17 4
- B. 194 31 46 8

- C. 195 31 50 4

- D. 196 31 63 9

- E 200 31 23 4

This lends the following conclusions.

- All the babies were born on different months

- All the babies were born on the 31st.

- Baby A and E were born before the baby in the example

We can rule out A and E as according to the information, baby A was born in the 192nd month and baby E in the 200th month since the first baby. This does not make logical sense, as they were born before the baby in the example.

We are now left with options B, C, D. They were all born in different months however, so the question here is asking us to look for months that have 31 days only.

If the 157th month is October, then;

- The 194th month will be 37 months after, therefore November (3 years and 1 month after)

- The 195th month will be 38 months after, therefore December

- The 196th month will be 39 months after, therefore January

- November only has 30 days, therefore, it can't be November.

- February has 28 days

We now rule out B and are left with C and D. Next, we should check that all of the values add up to what the last value represents.

C: 1 + 9 + 4 + 3 + 1 + 1 + 7 + 4 = 30 (Therefore 4 is the wrong last value)

D: 1 + 9 + 6 + 3 + 1 + 6 + 3 = 29 (Therefore 9 is the correct last value)

The answer is therefore D.

Answer: D

Expert's Advice!

Be tactical with your time, some questions take much longer than others. If it is going to take too long, skip it and come back at the end

Example Question 6:

Passage: Medic Mind is giving its employees a free drink to each of their mentors. Alice is working every day of the week but takes Saturday and Tuesday off. But to get this free drink he needs to use his Medic Mind Map. Each day she finishes mentoring, Alice gets 4 stamps on her map and she can use a certain number of these stamps for many things including a free drink. The number of stamps required for this drink does not change. On the morning of Sunday 3rd, Alice has 14 stamps on her map. She is always dehydrated and therefore tells herself that whenever she has the stamps, she will get the free drink. The first day that Alice is unable to get a drink is the 10th. Every day until then she buys one.

What day of the week will it be the second time she is unable to buy one?

A - Monday

B - Tuesday

C - Wednesday

D - Thursday

E - Friday

F - Saturday

G - Sunday

Explanation:

First of all, it is definite that the drink costs more than 4 stamps, as otherwise she would not run out of stamps. If it costs 5 stamps it is likely it would have taken slightly longer than a week to run out. Let us now assume it costs 6 stamps to buy a drink. On the 3rd, she starts with 14. She buys a drink it goes down to 8 but then she gets another 4 in the evening meaning she ends with 12. She therefore loses 2 tokens every day. This makes sense, as we are told that on the 8th, she does not have enough to buy the drink. Below shows how many stamps she starts off with every morning:

- Sunday 3rd - 14
- 4th - 12
- 5th (day off) -10
- 6th - 10
- 7th - 8
- 8th - 6
- 9th (Saturday no work) - 4
- 10th - 4
- 11th - 8
- 12th (Tuesday no work) - 6
- 13th - 6
- 14th - 4

The 14th will be the next day she is unable to buy the drink at work. This is a Thursday.

Answer: D

Take Home Points

1. **Shortcuts to date and time questions.** Learning key facts and tricks will save valuable time.
2. **Using working to answer questions.** When undertaking complex calculations making notes can help candidates solve problems more efficiently.
3. **Worked examples.** Worked Examples can help demonstrate shortcuts and tricks in problem solving questions.

1.9 Pin Code Questions

Pin Code questions fall under the *Problem Solving* component of the test. This type of question will present a series of clues and candidates will be required to deduce the pin code from the given information. This type of question often requires a trial and error approach and therefore, it is important to hone this skill in order to complete the questions quickly and accurately.

How to approach Pin Code Questions

Pin Code questions often require trial and error and there is no other way around them. Candidates will often be required to use algebra and other mathematical methods to help solve the problem. This type of question has appeared more frequently in recent years so honing this skill is strongly advised.

Example Question 1:

Passage:

A person has forgotten their 5-digit pin code but remembers some clues. The second digit is the square of the first digit The sum of the first and third digit is 10 The fourth digit is one more than the first digit The sum of the fifth and third digit equals 14

The sum of all the digits is 30

What is the first digit?

    A - 1

    B - 2

    C - 3

    D - 4

    E - 5

    F - 6

G – 7

Explanation:

Order the digits in alphabetic order, to assign variables to the 1st, 2nd, 3rd, 4th and 5th digits respectively as: 'a', 'b', 'c', 'd', 'e'.

'b' = 'a^2' (The second digit is the square of the 1st digit)

'a' + 'c'= 10 (The sum of the 1st and 3rd digits is 10)

Hence this equation can be re-written as c=10-'a' to express in terms of a

'd' = 'a' + 1 (the 4th digit is one more than the first digit)

'c' + 'e' = 14 (the sum of the 3rd and 5th digits equals 14), as 'c' = 10 - 'a', 'e' = 14 - (10 - 'a')

'a' + 'b' + 'c' + 'd' + 'e' = 30 (The sum of all digits is 30)

Sum of all digits can be expressed as:

'a'+ 'a^2' + (10 – 'a') + ('a' + 1) + 14 - (10 – 'a') = 30

Here, the + (10 – 'a') and –(10 – 'a') simply cancel, giving:

'a' + 'a^2' + ('a' + 1) + 14= 30

'a^2' + 2'a' + 15 = 30

'a^2' + 2'a'- 15 = 0

('a'+ 5) ('a' – 3) = 0

The 2 solutions are

1.   'a'=3
2.   'a' = -5

However, a pin code cannot have any negative numbers, so the accepted first   digit   is   3.

Answer: C

In these questions, candidates are also advised to use common sense alongside trial and error. For example, knowing that the second digit is a square of the first confirms that the first digit can only be between 1 and 3 as these are the only numbers with squares between the values of 0 and 9. Trial and error with these three options can quickly and efficiently help candidates reach the correct answer.

Expert's Advice!

Brush up on Algebra! As we just saw with the previous question, the algebraic method can be very helpful in approaching these questions. It is also often easier to work with algebraic calculations that are not complicated with numerical values.

Example Question 2:

> **Passage:** My 6-digit passcode for internet banking consists of six different digits. The second digit is 8. When the passcode is written as three 2-digit numbers, the three numbers add up to 170. The last digit is a prime number less than 5. When it is written as two 3-digit numbers, the two numbers add up to 1610.

What do the 1st and 4th numbers add up to?

> A -13
>
> B - 14
>
> C - 15
>
> D - 16
>
> E - 17

Explanation:

For these questions, always try to use algebra to achieve the correct answer. It often can take very long though, so trial and error may also work.

The question tells us that three 2-digit numbers add up to 1610, therefore, the second, fourth and sixth digits must add up to a multiple of 10.

Let 'x' be the 4th digit and y be the 6th digit.

- 8 + 'x' + 'y' = 10; this does not work as x and y have to be two different digits, and the only possibility is for 'x' and 'y' to both be 1 for the equation above to make sense.

- 8 + 'x' + 'y' = 20

- 'x' + 'y' = 12

'x' and 'y' therefore can be 5 and 7 or 3 and 9. They cannot be 4 and 8 as we already have 8. They also cannot be 6 and 6 as the two numbers have to be different from each other.

The question tells us that two 3-digit numbers add up to 170, therefore, the third and sixth digits must add up to a multiple of 10.

We said 'y' was the sixth digit, let 'z' be the 3rd digit. We have established that 'y' can either be 5, 7, 3 or 9.

'z' + 'y' = 10

'y' cannot be 5, as this would mean that 'z' would have to be 5 which is not possible as all numbers have to be different. 'y' cannot be 7 or 9 either as the last digit is a prime number less than 5

- 'y' = 3
- 'z' + 'y' = 10
- 'z' + 3 = 10
- 'z' = 7
- 'x' + 'y' = 12
- 'x' + 3 = 12
- 'x' = 9

Therefore,

- 'x' = 4th digit (9)

- 'y' = 6th digit (3)
- z' = 3rd digit (7)

Now, we know that

_ 8 7 9 _ 3

To find the first and fifth digits, we need to use the given information that the three numbers add up to 170. We know one of these three numbers is 79, therefore, the other two must add up to 91.

The only numbers remaining are 1, 2, 4, 6, 9

Three numbers add up to 170:

(i)8 + 78 + (j)3 = 170

(i)8 + (j)3 = 91

(i) and (j) must add up to 8 since 8 + 3 = 11.

Therefore, this means that either (i) = 2 and (j) = 6 or (i) = 6 and (j) = 2. Let's try both options. When (i) = 2 the pin code is 2 8 7 9 6 3. Therefore, the two 3-digit numbers are 287 and 963. Adding these numbers together gives us 1250 which is incorrect as the value should be 1610. Therefore, trying (i)=6 gives us a pin code of 6 8 7 9 2 3. Therefore, the two 3-digit numbers are 687 and 923. Adding these numbers together gives us 1610 which is correct. Therefore, the final sequence: 6 8 7 9 2 3.

The first number is 6, and the fourth number is 9 therefore they add up to 15. The answer is therefore C, 15

Answer: C

Common Trap

Be careful with your notations on your paper. It can be easy to make small mistakes when writing out equations and adding up numbers. Make sure to check your working - especially if your final answer does not match an answer option exactly.

Example Question 3:

Passage: Alice's pin code for her debit card has four digits which are all different from each other. When the number values are written out as words from the first to 4th number, they are all in alphabetical order. The first letter of each number denotes the alphabetical order. The first digit of Alice's pin is four and the last digit is three. None of the other two digits are square numbers

What is the total number of letters that make up the second and third digits?

A - 4

B - 6

C - 8

D - 10

E - 12

Explanation:

Let's begin by writing out the information given in the pin code.

4 _ _ 3

Also written as:

Four _ _ Three

We need two numbers in the middle that have a first letter between the letters 'fo' and 'th' when they are written out. We can, therefore, rule out some numbers.

- Two can be ruled out as it would come after Three in the alphabet.

- Five can be ruled out as it comes before Four in the alphabet.

- Eight can be ruled out as it comes before Four in the alphabet.

We are therefore left with One, Six Seven, Nine. We are told that none of the numbers are square numbers, which further rules out One and Nine.

The final code would therefore be:

4 7 6 3

or

4 6 7 3

We, therefore, need to add 5 (seven has five letters) and 3 (six has three letters), which gives us 8. The answer is therefore C, 8

Answer: C

It is important to maintain a methodical approach to this type of question. Use common sense to eliminate options and then work out the answer accordingly. Also note you may not be required to work out the entire pin code in order to select the answer, as seen in the example above.

Expert's Advice!

Always try and find any explicit information you have been told and work your way from there!

Example Question 4:

Passage: A dad is on holiday and has just gone swimming. He comes back and finds that his locker room isn't opening. He used his children's names to make the password. His children's names are: Salth, John, Aaron, Alex, Samuel, Lisa, David, Lawrence, Edgar, Fiona and Gareth. The swimming pool regulations state that you are not allowed to use the same name twice and two names must have at least four letters. It must also be in reverse alphabetical order The dad tries this: Samuel, Lawrence, John, David, Aaron. The lifeguard tells the dad that the password is wrong, and that the first, third and fourth names are in the correct position.

Which of the following is the correct combination to open the locker?

A- Samuel, Lisa, John, David, Alex

B - Salth, Lawrence, Gareth, Fiona, Edgar

C - Samuel, Kylian, John, David, Edgar

D - Samuel, Kylian, John, David, Alex

E - Samuel, Lisa, John, David, Fiona

Explanation:

We know this so far:

Samuel, _____ , John, David , _____

We know that we have these names to pick from: Salth, John, Aaron, Alex, Samuel, Lisa, David, Lawrence

We can rule out Samuel, John and David as they have already been picked

Salth, ~~John,~~ **Aaron, Alex,** ~~Samuel,~~ **Lisa,** ~~David,~~ **Lawrence**

We can also rule out Salth as we already have one name beginning with S.

~~Salth,~~ ~~John,~~ **Aaron, Alex,** ~~Samuel,~~ **Lisa,** ~~David,~~ **Lawrence**

We know that it is in reverse alphabetical order, therefore the fifth name has to be either Aaron or Alex. Aaron was tried and rejected. Therefore, the last name is Alex. We also know that it is in reverse alphabetical order, therefore the fourth name has to be either Lisa or Lawrence. Lawrence was tried and was rejected. Therefore, the second name is Lisa.

Therefore, this is the correct order:

Samuel, Lisa, John, David, Alex

Answer: A

Pin Code Questions can take some practice but honing the ability to complete the question quickly and accurately will improve your score on the day.

TAKE HOME POINTS

1. **Using algebra to answer pin code questions**. Algebra is often the most efficient method and will save valuable time.

2. **Reading the stem properly of the question**. The passages can be long, yielding the temptation to skim read. It is important to read these stems carefully to gather all the relevant information necessary.

3. **Worked examples.** Worked Examples can help demonstrate shortcuts and tricks in problem solving questions.

1.10 Ordered Questions

Ordered Questions fall under the *Problem Solving* component of the test. This type of question will present candidates with information on a group of individuals and candidates will be required to order them accordingly. This type of question tends to be one of the easier question formats in the problem solving component of the test. Therefore, practising this component of the test is essential to ensure you do not miss out on easy marks.

How to approach these questions

Ordered Questions require candidates to order a group of people or categories against a given criterion, such as weight or height. The ideal way to approach this format is to draw a table or list the information given in a more concise format than given in the question. The stem will often list information in a confusing and messy manner that, interestingly, mimics a lot of medical documentation. Try and order things from the most information to the most ambiguous and work out the required information accordingly, as you would be expected to do in a healthcare role.

Example Question 1

> **Passage**: Five marathon runners are having their weight measured before they run. Sarwath has a larger weight than Richard who has a larger weight than Madhi. Taher weighs less than Richard but weighs more than Aaron. Which of these people weigh more than Aaron?

Which of these people must weigh more than Aaron?

A - Richard, Madhi and Sarwath

B - Sarwath and Madhi, but not necessarily Richard

C - Madhi, but not necessarily Richard or Sarwath

D - Richard, but not necessarily Madhi or Sarwath

E - Sarwath and Richard, but not necessarily Madhi

Explanation:

This is an ordered question. We therefore need to be able to understand the positions of each person from heaviest to lightest.

Sarwath has a larger weight than Richard who has a larger weight than Madhi

S >R >M

Taher weighs less than Richard but weighs more than Aaron

R >T> A

From the information above, we know for a fact that Richard and Taher weigh more than Aaron. We also know that Sarwath weighs more than Richard meaning Sarwath will also weigh more than Aaron. With Madhi, we know that Richard has a larger weight than her, however, she could still have a weight that is lower than Aaron's. In other words, we do not yet know where M will fit within the list. Is she between R and T, T and A or after A?

The answer is therefore E, Richard and Sarwath, but not necessarily Madhi.

Answer: E

Expert's Advice!

Always start with the most obvious information as a starting point and go from there! An easy way to denote this information will be to use alphabets or numerical values as this saves valuable time and helps reduce confusion.

Example Question 2:

Passage: The draw for the knock-out stages of the Champions of England Tournament took place recently. The teams are numbered on the right. The first drawn team plays the second drawn team. The third drawn team plays the fourth drawn team and the fifth drawn team plays the sixth drawn team. The same occurs for the seventh and eighth team drawn.

Several observations were made. Each ball that was drawn was followed by an odd number when it was even and was followed by an even number when it was odd. There was also a difference of three between each team i.e. between Liverpool and their opponent, and Manchester City and their opponent.

This rule is not applied to Arsenal.

The last ball that was drawn was for Manchester City (5). The first ball that was drawn was for Liverpool (6). What will the two fixtures be?

A - Manchester City v Blackburn and Liverpool v Leicester

B - Manchester City v Manchester Utd and Liverpool v Leicester

C - Manchester City v Blackburn and Liverpool v Chelsea

D - Manchester City v Everton and Liverpool v Chelsea

Explanation:

First of all, we know that the last number was odd, therefore, the second last number has to be even. It also must have a difference of three from the number 5; thus, the team playing Manchester City must be either 8 or 2. Maintaining a difference of three between teams means that if the 7th team was 8, then the 6th team would either have to be 5 or 11. It can't be 5 as there is already a number 5 and it cannot be 11 as there is no number 11. This rules out 8 and leaves us with 2. We therefore know that the team playing Manchester City is number 2, which is Blackburn. We knock-out B and D

We also know that the first number was even, therefore the second number must be odd. It also must have a difference of three from the number 6 therefore the team playing Liverpool has to be either 9 or 3. There is no number 9, therefore, the number is 3. We know for sure that Liverpool are playing the number 3 which is Leicester. We can knock-out C. This process of elimination leaves us with the answer A.

Answer: A

Common Trap

Avoid attempting these questions without using notations. Often, candidates will attempt to peruse the information in its true form, as given in the stem. This leads to mistakes, confusion and often, a large amount of time wased. Note the relevant information down for increased efficiency and accuracy.

Example Question 3

> Passage: Joseph, Sam, James, John and Tim are all a group of friends, and are entering into a rugby tournament. Their surnames are Jarn, Sult, Tun, Lisca, and Hirth. They have to fill in each others surnames and are told only one thing. In their full names no letter of the alphabet appears twice in their first name and second name combined. The last name of each friend has a different number of letters from their first name and their first name cannot start with the same letter as their second name.

What is John's surname?

  A - Jarn

  B - Sult

  C - Tun

  D - Lisca

  E - Hirth

Explanation:

Firstly, we are told that the last names for each friend have a different number of letters from their first name. A good idea, therefore, would be to begin by spotting the number of letters in each first name.

Number of letters in first name		Number of letters in second name	
3	Tim, Sam	3	Tun
4	John	4	Jarn, Sult
5	Joseph, James	5+	Hirth, Lisca

This helps us understand what possible second names each person can have. We are told that the first letter of each name has to be different to the corresponding surname. We are also told that the two names cannot have the same letters.

We are looking for John's surname. It cannot be Jarn or Sult as they both have four letters. It can, however, be Tun, Hirth or Lisca. Since it can be one of three options, it would be best to try and match these three surnames with the other characters.

Sam has to have the surname Hirth as Sult begins with 'S' and both, Jarn and Lisca, has an 'a'. So now, John could be either Tun or Lisca. No one else can be Lisca, as Joseph and James both have 5 letters and the only other candidate is Tim but his name has the letter 'i'. Therefore, John's surname is Lisca.

Answer: D

Expert's Advice!

Only solve the puzzle as far as required. Upon completion of each step in the puzzle, check to see if you have arrived at the answer. This is to ensure that you do not fall into the trap of completing the entire puzzle before picking an answer. This will help save time in the BMAT.

Example Question 4:

Passage: Aaron enters a competition where he has to guess the number of people in a picture. He came third in the competition and here are the results from the leader board.

Position	Name	Guess
1st	Daniel	60
2nd	Mark	75
3rd	Aaron	77
4th	Lisa	56
5th	Elizabeth	55

What was the actual number of people?

    A - 64

    B - 65

    C - 66

    D - 67

    E - 68

    F - 69

Explanation:

With this question, you should take each answer option and see how far away it is from each value.

Let's start with 64.

- 1st - 4 away
- 2nd - 11 away
- 3rd - 13 away
- 4th - 9 away

We can stop here as we know this does not follow the pattern we require. It therefore cannot be 64 but is going to be greater than 64 as we need a number that is further away from 56 than it is from 77. We know the number has to be three more than 64, as this will mean it is only 10 away from the 3rd and 11 away from the 4th.

Adding 3 to 64 gives us 67. Let's try 67

- 1st - 7 away
- 2nd - 8 away
- 3rd - 10 away
- 4th - 11 away
- 5th - 12 away

We therefore know that the answer is D, 67.

Answer: D

TAKE HOME POINTS

1. **Making notes to answer problem solving.** Reducing information into a condensed form makes processing it faster.

2. **Focusing on the task and not getting distracted.** Deduce the relevant information and disregard the rest - be efficient with your time.

3. **Worked examples** - these demonstrate helpful tips and tricks for faster problem solving.

1.11 Speed, Distance & Time

Speed, Distance and Time Questions fall under the *Problem Solving* component of the test. This type of question will present information and candidates will be required to use the relevant equations to calculate the answer.

How to approach these questions

In order to effectively complete these questions candidates must be familiar with the following foundational formulae.

- Speed = Distance / Time
- Distance = Speed x Time
- Time = Distance / Speed
- Acceleration (m/s²) = Change in Velocity / Time Taken

For example, a car takes 5 seconds to accelerate from 25m/s to 35m/s. This equates to a change in velocity of 10m/s as the difference between 35 and 25 is 10. Using the formula for acceleration we know that this change in velocity of 10m/s must be divided by the time of 5 seconds. Overall, this demonstrates that the acceleration is 2m/s². On a speed-time graph, the gradient will be equal to the acceleration. So, a rising line means a constant acceleration and an increasing speed. The distance is the area under the graph. See the graph below for a visual representation.

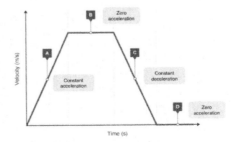

Speed and velocity are very similar concepts. Speed is the time rate at which an object is moving along a path, while velocity is the rate and direction of an object's movement. For simplicity, candidates can envision that Velocity = Speed + Direction.

Candidates are advised to read the question and passage. They must then substitute information into the equations above to correctly deduce the answer to the question.

Common Trap

Be careful with the units. Often changing units create a trap!
For example, speed distance time calculations must be done in line with the question format of meters per second. Therefore, if the question presents the information in minutes and the distance in meters make sure to convert the time into seconds.

Example Question 1:

> Passage: At London Euston, both the Northern and Victoria lines have connections to it. So do Warren Street and Kings Cross. In between these stations there is a single-track railway. The Victoria Line services leaves Kings Cross station at 13:14 and travels at an average speed of 20 km/h in between stations. The Northern line leaves Warren Street at 13:14 and travels at an average speed of 40 km/h. The distance between Euston Station and Warren Street is 30km. The distance between Kings Cross and Euston is 10km. In order to regulate the service, each train must wait at Euston for at least 7 minutes.

What is the earliest time for the Victoria Line to arrive at Warren Street if it starts at Kings Cross at 13:14?

    A - 13:49

    B - 14:29

    C - 14:49

    D - 15:19

    E - 15:29

Explanation:

The distance between Kings Cross and Warren Street is 40km. This is because the distance from Warren Street to Euston is 30km and the distance from Euston to Kings Cross is 10km. The Victoria Line from King's Cross travels at 20 km/h. The Northern Line from Warren Street, however, travels at 40km/h.

Both trains will cross, however, they can only intersect inside Euston station when they are stationary, i.e. waiting for passengers. This is because there is only one single-track railway on the journey whereas Euston Station has platforms for many trains.

Let's calculate the time each train takes to reach Euston Station

Time = Distance / Speed

- Northern Line: Warren Street —> Euston: 30/40 = 0.75 hours = 45 minutes
- Victoria Line: Kings Cross —> Euston: 10/20 = 0.5 hours = 30 minutes

Therefore, the Northern Line arrives at 13:59 while the Victoria Line arrives much earlier, at 13:44. However, Victoria Line will have to wait until Northern Line has entered Euston before it can move as it is a single-track railway.

At 13:59, Victoria Line can continue its journey to Warren Street. Thereafter, travelling from Euston to Warren Street will take 1.5 hours. This means that the Victoria Line will arrive at 15:29. The answer is therefore E, 15:29

Note: The 7 minutes of waiting time for the Victoria Train is not relevant to the calculations, as the arrival of the Northern Line exceeds the waiting time. The Northern Line arrives at 13:59, which is 15 minutes of waiting time from the arrival of the Victoria Line, inclusive of the 7 minutes. The 7 minutes of waiting do not make any difference for the Northern Line, as the Victoria Line has to leave immediately, upon its arrival.

Answer: E

Expert's Advice!

Drawing a quick diagram of the different items can be helpful. For example, in the question above it may be helpful to draw out a line with KX (kings cross) at one end, E (Euston in the middle) and WS (Warren Street) at the end. Visualising the problem not only makes it quicker to solve but also may help candidates pick up on common traps like the single-track railway above.

Example Question 2:

Passage: Euston Station also has trains from different areas in the UK. Each train runs both ways to and from Euston to its respective destination

Each train to Euston departs on the hour e.g. 09:00, 10:00. Each train departs from Euston half past the hour e.g. 9:30, 10:30. The journey times are shown on the graph.

Each regional train i.e. Luton —> Leicester and Leicester —>

Manchester run at 50 past e.g. 09:50, 10:50

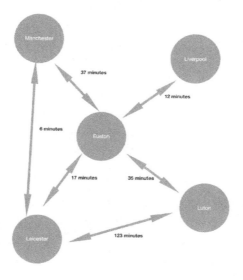

If I get to Luton station at 15:44 and I take the quickest route including waiting times, what time will I get to Manchester?

A - 18:07

B - 17:56

C - 18:14

D - 17:44

E - 17:58

Explanation:

There are four ways to get to Manchester from Luton.

- **Option 1:** Luton —> Euston —> Manchester
- **Option 2:** Luton —> Euston —> Leicester —> Manchester
- **Option 3:** Luton —> Leicester —> Euston —> Manchester
- **Option 4:** Luton —> Leicester —> Manchester

Option 3 is clearly not feasible as it takes far longer than the other trains, even if they involve waiting times of up to an hour.

If she gets to Luton station at 15:44, she can get a train at 16:00

If she goes to Euston, she will get there at 16:35. This means she has to wait another 55 minutes for a train at 17:30, and she has two options from Euston:

- **Option 1:** Going directly to Manchester —> she would get to Manchester at 18:07.

- **Option 2:** Going via Leicester- she would get to Leicester at 17:47 and would get the train at 17:50 to get there for 17:56

She also has one other option via Leicester and straight to Manchester

- **Option 4:** If she goes to Leicester, she will get the train at 15:50, and she will get to Leicester at 17:53. She will miss the 17:50 train straight to Manchester.

Her best option is therefore Option 2.

Answer B

Expert's Advice!

Occasionally questions may be presented in the kilometres per hour (km/h) format. If this is the case, ensure to covert all times into hours and all distances into kilometres. In the case of minutes then multiply by 60. In the case of meters divide by 1000.

Example Question 3

Passage: To get from Euston to City Airport, there is a bus that many people catch. This bus takes 40 minutes in both directions. The timetable for the bus is shown on the right. Serena lives within walking distance of Euston station and always goes on the bus when she wants to pick up her family from the airport. Her brother is coming from Toronto on Sunday, and she wants to stay in the airport and shop at duty free as long as she can. However, she needs to be back to Euston before 18:00.

When she gets to the airport, her brother had already landed 30 minutes ago. He left Toronto at 01:30 Canadian Time and his flight was 7 hours. Canada is 5 hours behind the UK.

Departures from Euston Station						
Mon	Tues	Wed	Thurs	Fri	Sat	Sun
09:00	8:00	11:00	09:00	8:00	10:10	12:20
09:30	9:00	13:00	09:30	9:00	11:10	13:20
10:00	10:00	15:00	10:00	10:00	12:10	14:40
10:30	11:00	17:00	10:30	11:00	13:10	15:40
11:00	12:00		11:00	12:00	14:10	16:40
11:30	13:00		11:30	13:00	15:10	17:00
12:00	14:00		12:00	14:00		17:20
	15:00			15:00		

Departures from Airport						
Mon	Tues	Wed	Thurs	Fri	Sat	Sun
8:00	11:00	09:00	8:00	8:00	10:10	10:10
9:00	13:00	09:30	9:00	9:00	11:10	11:10
10:00	15:00	10:00	10:00	10:00	12:10	12:10
11:00	17:00	10:30	11:00	11:00	13:10	13:10
12:00		11:00	12:00	12:00	14:10	14:10
13:00		11:30	13:00	13:00	15:10	15:10
14:00		12:00	14:00	14:00		16:10
15:00			15:00	15:00		17:10

What time did she meet her brother?

A - 08:30

B - 13:30

C - 14:00

   D – 15:00

   E - 16:30

Explanation:

Her brother landed at 08:30, according to Canadian Time. In the UK, this corresponds to 13:30. Therefore, she met her brother at 14:00. She got on the bus which left at 13:20. This is as he was waiting for 30 minutes – 14:00, and the bus takes 40 minutes – 14:00.

This question was filled with excessive and unnecessary information. Reading the question first can help filter through the information to find the relevant facts.

Answer: C

Common Trap

If a question talks about travelling somewhere and coming back, do not forget to double the distance!

Example Question 4:

Passage: Serena's brother, Raju is living at Endsleigh Court and likes to explore the nearby facilities. He normally walks to Soho and he walks at a pace of 4km/h. Serena is not fond of walking as she finds it boring. So, she hires a bike. She normally overtakes Raju at Oxford Circus. Raju left 30 minutes after Serena, and managed to overtake Serena outside Tottenham Court Road, which is 4km from Oxford Circus.

What speed does Serena cycle?

   A - 4 km/h

   B - 6 km/h

   C - 8 km/h

   D - 10 km/h

Explanation:

4 km from Oxford Circus is the distance when Raju leaves 30 minutes late. This means that when Raju leaves on time, he is 2 km from Oxford Circus. This is because he walks at a speed of 4km/h. Therefore in 30 minutes, he will have covered 2 km, leaving 2 km left to reach his destination.

Since they usually meet at Oxford Circus, Serena has to cover 2km while Raju covers 2km as well. This, therefore, means she cycles at the same speed that Raju walks. The answer is therefore A, 4 km/h.

Answer: A

Expert's Advice!

If you struggle to remember the formula you can always use the triangle. The triangle can be seen below.

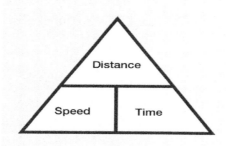

This triangle demonstrates that distance is equal to the product of speed and time. Similarly, it can be seen that speed is equal to distance over time i.e distance/time. Analogously, it can be seen that time is equal to distance over speed i.e distance/speed.

Example Question 5:

> **Passage:** There are two joggers who are going through Regents Park. Jogger 1's top speed is 12km/h and Jogger 2's top speed is   8km/h.

If both are running at top speed in a straight line, and Jogger 1 is 500 m behind, how many seconds will it take for Jogger 1 to catch Jogger 2?

    A - 0.125

    B - 7.5

    C - 450

    D - 600

    E - 1000

Explanation:

First of all, we are told Jogger 1 runs at a speed of 12km/h whilst Jogger 2 runs at a speed of 8 km/h. Therefore, the speed difference is 4km/h. We are told the distance difference is 0.5km therefore we must work out the time.

- Time = Distance Difference / Speed Difference
- X = 0.5/4
- X = 0.125 hours
- X = 7.5 minutes
- X = 450 seconds

Answer: C

TAKE HOME POINTS

1.   **Tackling tricky speed distance time questions**. Filter for relevant information and try drawing out diagrams to make the question easier.

2.   **Becoming familiar with relevant selection questions.** Trains and bus timetables are very common formats so familiarise yourself with   these   question   types.

1.12 Tabular Questions

Tabular Questions fall under the *Problem Solving* component of the test. This type of question will present a table and some accompanying information; candidates will be required to perform calculations with this information to work out the correct answer. This type of question often presents an excess of information and requires candidates to identify the relevant information quickly and effectively. This is an important skill for future medics to possess as often patient histories contain large amounts of information. Doctors are required to sift through this to identify the necessary data for fast and accurate diagnosis.

How to approach these questions

It is advised to read the question before the passage in order to garner an idea of the relevant information that will be required. Next it is advisable to read the passage and identify the key details. Finally, candidates are advised to apply the correct mathematical procedures to successfully work out the answer.

Example Question 1:

Passage: Here is a metric table which looks specifically at BMI. At school they are measuring each Year 5 pupil's BMI. The combined weight of Kalar, Mac and Anu is 150 kg. Mac is 136 cm tall and has a BMI of 27. Kalar has a BMI of 23 and has a height of 129 cm. Anu has a height of 160 cm.

	Underweight			Normal						Overweight					Obese					
BMI	16	17	18	19	20	21	22	23	24	25	26	27	28	29	30	31	32	33	34	35
Height (cm)	Body Weight (kg)																			
145	34	36	38	40	42	44	46	48	50	53	55	57	59	61	63	65	67	69	71	74
150	36	38	41	43	45	47	50	52	54	56	59	61	63	65	68	70	72	74	77	79
155	38	41	43	46	48	50	53	55	58	60	62	65	67	70	72	74	77	79	82	84
160	41	44	46	49	51	54	56	59	61	64	67	69	72	74	77	79	82	84	87	90
165	44	46	49	52	54	57	60	63	65	68	71	74	76	79	82	84	87	90	93	95
170	46	49	52	55	58	61	64	66	69	72	75	78	81	84	87	90	92	95	98	101
175	49	52	55	58	61	64	67	70	74	77	80	83	86	89	92	95	98	101	104	107
180	52	55	58	62	65	68	71	75	78	81	84	87	91	94	97	100	104	107	110	113
185	55	58	62	65	68	72	75	79	82	86	89	92	96	99	103	106	110	113	116	120
190	58	61	65	69	72	76	79	83	87	90	94	97	101	105	108	112	116	119	123	126
195	61	65	68	72	76	80	84	87	91	95	99	103	106	110	114	118	122	125	129	133
200	64	68	72	76	80	84	88	92	96	100	104	108	112	116	120	124	128	132	136	140

What is Anu's BMI?

A - 24

B - 26

C - 28

D - 30

E - 32

F - 34

Explanation:

From the information given we can start by working out the weight of Mac and Kalar.

BMI = Weight/Height^2

Note: Height is in metres for BMI calculations

To find Mac's weight,

$27 = M/(1.36^2)$

$\therefore M = 27 \times (1.362^2)$

M $=$ 49.9 kg

To find Kalar's weight, we do the same thing

$23 = K/(1.292^2)$

K = 38.3 kg

Since their combined weights are 150 kg, we can do

150 - (38.3 + 49.9) = 61.8 kg

We know his height is 1.6m, so to find his BMI, use the aforementioned equation.

$61.8/1.6^2 = 24.14$

Answer: A

TIMING TIP

Sometimes, if the question itself is 2-3 lines, it's worth reading that before reading the stem or answer options.

Example Question 2:

Passage: The table below shows the different number of rugby players at different levels for the red team and blue team in the Bulldog League. There is a probability of 1 in 10 that a red team player selected at random, is a junior level player.

	Reds	Blues	Total
First Team	11	13	
U23s		22	25
U21s			20
U18s	4		
Junior Level			25
Total		60	100

How many Blues are there at junior level?

    A - 13

    B - 15

    C - 17

    D - 19

    E - 21

Explanation:

First, we fill in all the information we can on the table.

	Reds	Blues	Total
First Team	11	13	24
U23s	3	22	25
U21s			20
U18s	4	2	6
Junior Level			25
Total	40	60	100

We know that there is a probably of 1 in 10 that a red team player selected at random is at junior level, and there are 40 reds therefore there are 4 at junior level.

	Reds	Blues	Total
First Team	11	13	24
U23s	3	22	25
U21s			20
U18s	4	2	6
Junior Level	4		25
Total	40	60	100

We therefore know that there are 21 blues at junior level as there are 25 junior level players in total and 4 of them are red.

Answer: E

Expert's Advice!

Read tables in an L. It's easy to get caught up into reading all parts of a table but if you read it in an L, you'll spot what the data falls under.

Example Question 3

The table below shows Alex's body fat composition (%) and muscle mass (kg) recording at different times over a week.

Day	Time	Body fat composition (%)	Muscle mass (kg)	Calorie Count
Monday	12pm	22	44	66
Monday	3pm	22	46	68
Monday	6pm	23	43	67
Monday	9pm	23	41	65
Tuesday	12pm	22	47	64
Tuesday	3pm	22	44	66
Tuesday	6pm	21	45	66
Tuesday	9pm	23	49	67
Wednesday	12pm	23	44	68
Wednesday	3pm	21	45	65
Wednesday	6pm	22	45	66
Wednesday	9pm	22	46	67
Thursday	12pm	23	47	67
Thursday	3pm	21	43	67
Thursday	6pm	23	44	65
Thursday	9pm	21	45	66

What was Alex's calorie count on the measurement that had the highest discrepancy between body fat composition and muscle mass?

A - 64

B - 65

C - 66

D - 67

E - 68

Explanation:

To answer this question, we need to look for largest difference between body fat composition and muscle mass. A good way to do this would be to look for the lowest body fat composition measurement and highest muscle mass measurement.

On four separate occasions, body fat composition is 21%.

Tuesday	6pm	21	45
Wednesday	3pm	21	45
Thursday	3pm	21	43
Thursday	9pm	21	45

The greatest difference here is at 6pm Tuesday, 3pm Wednesday, Thursday 9pm (24). On one occasion the weight is 49kg.

Tuesday	9pm	23	49

The greatest difference here is Tuesday 9pm (26). The answer therefore is D - 67.

Answer: D

Expert's Advice!

Don't miss the data next to the table. Don't ignore whatever information the table comes with!

Example Question 4

Passage: UCL Medical School is making their timetable for their first-year students. There are three main lecturers and there are exactly two lectures per day. All professors work three times a week except Thursdays. None of the lecturers are allowed to work three days in a row.

	Monday	Tuesday	Wednesday	Thursday	Friday
Professor Delves	✔		✔		✔
Professor Anderson	✔	✔		✔	
Professor Dean	✘	✔	✔		✔

Which of the following days are Professor Anderson and Professor Dean working on the same day?

    A - Monday

    B - Tuesday

    C - Wednesday

    D - Thursday

    E - Friday

Explanation:

For this question, we need to use the information that we are presented with and try and fill in the table.

We know that Professor Delves and Professor Anderson must both work on Monday since Professor Dean can't work on Monday.

Next, we know that we need at least two people working everyday. This means that both Professor Delves and Professor Dean have to come in on Wednesday and Friday as Professor Anderson only works three times a week.

	Monday	Tuesday	Wednesday	Thursday	Friday
Professor Delves	✔		✔		✔
Professor Anderson	✔	✔		✔	
Professor Dean	✘		✔		✔

The only other day that Professor Dean works has to be Tuesday, as he can't work three days in a row. Therefore, the answer is B.

	Monday	Tuesday	Wednesday	Thursday	Friday
Professor Delves	✔		✔		✔
Professor Anderson	✔	✔		✔	
Professor Dean	✘	✔	✔		✔

Answer: B

Example Question 5:

Passage: In the women's rugby league, there are four teams and all play each other once, at a neutral ground. A win gives each team 3 points, a draw gives each team 1 point and a loss gives each team 0 points. This is the league table at the end of the season.

Team	Points
Harlequins	4
Saracens	9
Ospreys	0
Bulls	4

What did Harlequin do against Bulls?

    A - Win

    B - Draw

    C - Loss

    D - There is insufficient information.

Explanation:

We know that Harlequins and Bulls both got 4 points. In order to achieve 4 points, they must have drawn one game, won the second game and lost the third game. There is no other way to achieve 4 points in the season.

Both their wins have to have come from beating Ospreys, as Ospreys got no points and so, lost all their games.

This means that they drew with each other. The answer is therefore B.

Answer: B

TAKE HOME POINTS

1.   **Answering tabular BMAT questions.** Take an efficient approach, filter out key information to solve problems quickly and accurately.

2.   **Common Traps and timing techniques.** Read the question first and read tables in an L shape.

1.13 Mathematical Reasoning

Mathematical Reasoning Questions fall under the *Problem Solving* component of the test. This type of question will present candidates with information and candidates will be required to perform calculations with this information to work out the correct answer.

Mathematical Reasoning Questions

For these questions, candidates will be required to utilise skills of inspection to try and answer questions in the short time frame allocated. These questions place a greater focus on problem solving abilities instead of mathematical abilities - due to the latter being tested in Section 2. Thus, instead of involving complex mathematical calculations, this component of the test is geared towards efficient information processing and use of mathematical logic. The following pages will outline key examples of this question type that appear most frequently in the paper.

Example Question 1

> **Passage**: Alan is inter-railing around Europe and was unable to purchase a ticket. This ticket gives you access to the entire railing network in Europe, and so he has to purchase individual tickets. He comes across a special offer from PersonalTrain: First two train tickets - €20 each. Third and subsequent tickets - €15 each
>
> PersonalTrain also gave him a finder's offer as his friend is also inter-railing. This means that, if he buys 10 tickets, he will pay €15 for all of his tickets. This includes the first 2, which would have otherwise been €20. To upgrade to first class, he needs to pay an extra €2 per ticket or €15 if he buys 10 first-class tickets. Alan has decided to purchase 5 first-class tickets. His friend, Steve who also has the finder's offer is purchasing 10 standard tickets. They are the only two people travelling.

How much more is Steve paying than Alan in total?

    A - €40

    B - €45

    C - €50

    D - €55

Explanation:

This passage contains a large volume of information, but the question is actually quite simple. We need to work out how much Alan is paying and how much Steve is paying.

Alan

Alan doesn't qualify for the finder's offer as he purchases 5 tickets. He pays €40 (€20 x 2) in total for the first two train tickets. For the third, fourth and fifth he pays €45 (€15 x 3) in total. He also has gone for first class and so has to pay €10 euros additionally.

€40 + €45 + €10 = €95

Steve

Steve qualifies for the finder's offer as he purchases 10 tickets. He therefore pays €150 as the first two tickets are €15.

€150 - €95 = €55

Answer is therefore D, €55.

Answer: D

Expert's Advice!

Don't be overwhelmed by the amount of information! Read the question so you can quickly identify the relevant information and disregard the rest. If it is not going to help you find the correct answer, you don't need to know it!

Example Question 2:

Passage: Conor McGregor is calculating how much tax will be deducted from his earnings, all gained from his UFC fights. He has to pay different amounts of tax depending on how many fights he has had. For his fight in 2015, Conor McGregor had to pay £6,000 on his fight. For his fight in 2017 with Floyd Mayweather, he paid £300 less than he paid in 2015, despite the fact that he made £3,000 more.

Number of fights	Less than 10	10 and more
Tax free	£0 – £10,000	£0 – £13,000
20%	£10,000 – £20,000	£13,000 – £24,000
30%	£20,000 +	£24,000 +

How much did Conor make from his fight with Floyd Mayweather to the nearest thousand?

    A - £34,000

    B - £35,000

    C - £36,000

    D - £37,000

Explanation:

This is slightly more complicated than a usual taxation question. It's clear from the start, that the fight in 2015 was his ninth one. His fight in 2017 was his 10th fight, as there is no other plausible explanation as to why he was paying more.

Therefore, we know that he paid £5,700 in tax in his fight in 2017. However, we don't know how much he has paid in each bracket.

The maximum he can pay in the 20% bracket is £2,200.

£24,000 - £13,000 = £11,000

20% of £11,000 is £2,200

He therefore is paying the remainder in the 30% bracket. We need to work out this remainder.

£5,700 - £2,200 = £3,500

£3,500 represents 30%

Let x be 100% amount

0.3x=3500

x=3500/0.3 = 11,666.666

He, therefore, earned £24,000 (since he paid the maximum he could have paid in the first two brackets in tax) and £9,833 from the third bracket.

£24,000 + £11,666 = £35,666

Round £35,666 up to £36,000

Answer: C

TIMING TIP!

Don't get caught up in trying to answer the question, if you can't answer it, guess and move on. Spending ages trying to find the answer is not an efficient use of your precious time. If you cannot work out a way to solve the problem, then make an educated guess and move on. This time will be much better spent answering questions you know how to approach and solve.

Example Question 3:

Passage: Brendan is laying out cones for his football training session at Liverpool. He has lots of cones, and so does not bother to count them but lays them out on the ground as a square grid. Once he has completed this square, he finds that he still has 4 cones left over. Brendan questions his character, and so lays them out again with one extra cone on either side of his grid. He then finds out that he is 13 cones short.

How many cones does he have?

A - 8

B - 28

C - 48

D - 68

E - 88

Explanation:

$x^2 + 4 = (x + 1)^2 - 13$

$x^2 + 4 = x^2 + 2x + 1 - 13$

$x^2 + 4 = x^2 + 2x - 12$

$4 = 2x - 12$

$16 = 2x$

$8 = x$

To find out how many cones he has in total we need to use the first equation,

$x2 + 4$

$(8)^2 + 4 = 68$

Answer: D

Example Question 4:

Passage: Sam is at a family wedding reception and is sat at a table with 13 other girls and 14 boys. Of the boys on the table, three older boys have younger brothers at the table, and two other boys have sisters on the table. Of the girls on the table, 4 older girls have younger sisters on the table, and 2 other girls have brothers on the table.

If there are no twins, and no family has more than two children who are attending the wedding, how many of the children on the table do not have either a brother or sister on the table?

A - 7

B - 8

C - 9

D – 10

Explanation:

For this question, it is clear that the information needs to be presented in a more accessible and understandable format.

- 3 boys that have 3 younger brothers
- 2 boys that have 2 sisters
- 4 girls that have 4 younger sisters
- 2 girls that have 2 brothers

It is clear that the 2 boys that have 2 sisters and the 2 girls that have 2 brothers are the same group of 4. That means that there are 18 people that have siblings.

There are 28 people in total, including Sam. We now find out the number that don't have siblings.

28 - 18 = 10

Answer: D

Example Question 5:

Passage: Matthew is a librarian, who is stacking a few shelves. He comes across one shelf which cannot hold more than 500g of books, with an allowance of no more than 5g heavier or lighter. Each shelf can hold 5 books. There were 6 books that were left to shelf, and these weighed 123g, 99g, 96g, 93g, 110g, 94g. He managed to fill the shelf to the allowance, but one book was left over.

What was the weight of the book that was left over?

  A - 123g

  B -101g

  C - 96g

  D - 110g

  E - 94g

Explanation:

A great way to approach this question is to work out the difference of each book to 100g, as this is the average weight each book should be since 100g x 5 = 500g. When we add all the differences from 100g, we want them to be within the range of +5g and -5g.

+23, -1, -4, -7, +10, -6.

This is only possible with:

+23, -7, -4, -1, -6 which gives a difference of +5g.

Therefore, we leave the book of size 110g. The answer is therefore D.

Answer: D

Expert's Advice!

Trial and error is a useful method to use when you get stuck! In the case of the question above, it is hard to judge which combination of books will fall within the range. Trial and error can help guide you to the right answer. For example, if one combination is too heavy, it guides you towards choosing a lighter combination.

TAKE HOME POINTS

1. **Use Algebra when appropriate**. Algebra saves valuable time therefore, implementing it where appropriate is advised.
2. **Common Traps and timing techniques**. Filter out the excess information and focus solely on information pertaining to the question. If a question is taking too long, guess it and move on.

1.14 Cube Questions

Cube Questions fall under the *Problem Solving* component of the test. This type of question will present visual information about a cube, and candidates will be required to deduce information about the cube, in order to select the correct answer. This type of question requires a high degree of abstract reasoning and visualisation skills.

How to Approach Cube Questions

In this type of question, candidates will be given a cube or a net of a 3-dimensional cube which contains unique digits, symbols or other markings on each face. Candidates will be required to identify the

- Cube created from the net shown
- Opposite face of a cube from 3 views shown
- Unfolded pattern which makes up the 3D cube displayed.

The best way to answer these questions is to try and visualise the cube if presented with a net or try and visualise its other faces. Candidates are advised to use a process of elimination to try and rule out possibilities that cannot occur for sure.

Example Question 1:

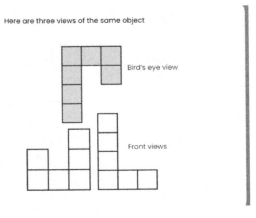

Here are three views of the same object

Bird's eye view

Front views

Which of the figures correspond to these elevations?

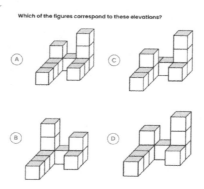

Explanation:

This question is all about elimination. From the bird's eye view, we can see that this is a U-shaped pattern. We can also see there should be 4 squares on the left and 2 on the right. Most of the shapes in the answers fit this pattern except for the shape in Answer Option A. There are 4 squares on the left but **3** on the right, so A is therefore incorrect.

The U shape shows that the correct shape should be one with 2 high on the left and 3 high on the right. Answer Option C and D fit this pattern but answer option B is 3 high on the right and 2 high on the left. Therefore, B is incorrect.

Looking at the front view on the right, we can see that it is L-shaped. None of the remaining shapes look L shaped, so we can assume this has been rotated. Indeed, it seems to represent that the shape is 3 high and 2 long. Now both C and D meet this criterion.

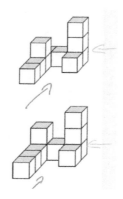

But remember that we are looking at the shape from where the yellow arrows are pointing. The only difference between C and D is one cube. It is the one circled on both C and D. In C, it sits slightly forward and in D it sits right at the back. This means that in C it would be visible but in D it would be hidden by the cubes that the yellow arrow is pointing at. In the front view that is L shaped, the circled cube is missing, which means that we can eliminate answer option C and therefore, answer option D is correct.

Answer: D

Expert's Advice!

Elimination is key! Ruling out answers that are obviously wrong first will allow more time to investigate the remaining answer options. This will save valuable time by helping you find the correct answer more quickly.

Example Question 2:

The same cube is shown below with three different views.

Which shape is opposite the paperclip?

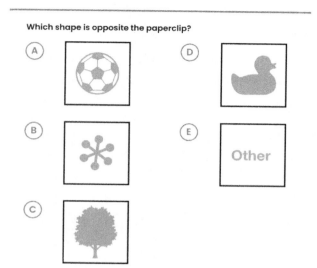

Explanation:

With this question, we have been given 3 views of the same cube and it's important to look for commonalities with those views. The duck and snowflake patterns are present in cube 1 and again in cube 3. The only difference is that in the latter, the pattern has been rotated 90 degrees anticlockwise. This means that the paper clip is now coming into vision, whilst the tree has disappeared from view.

This means that the paper clip must be positioned on the side where the yellow arrow is pointing, opposite the tree, so that when the paper clip turns into view, the tree turns out of view. Therefore, when we look at the answer options, we can choose answer option C, the tree, as the correct answer, as this is the shape which is opposite the paper clip.

Answer: C

Expert's Advice!

Switching between 3D and 2D visualisations can be difficult. Be sure to make note of what faces are next to each other on the sides of the shape you can see.

Example Question 3:

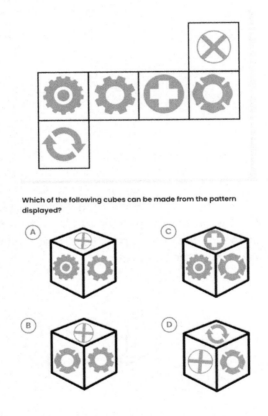

Which of the following cubes can be made from the pattern displayed?

Explanation:

With these net style questions, it's important to pick a reference point. Typically, the top of the cube is a good reference point. In answer Option A, we can see that there is a circle with a cross in it, at the top of the cube, so we can keep this as the constant.

The circle with a cross on the top of the cube. The petal shape folds underneath.

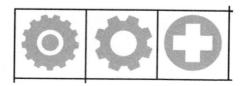

Each of these sides folds around the cube.

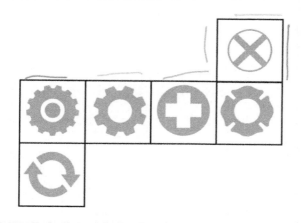

The two sides lined in green will oppose each other, the two sides lined in yellow will oppose each other and finally, the two sides lined in purple will oppose each other. The recycling sign will flap underneath, to form the floor of the cube.

Answer options C and D can be eliminated because they don't show the circle with a cross at the top of the cube. Answer option B can also be eliminated because it does not match the pattern in the net.

Answer option A, shows the circle with a cross at the top, and the gears next to each other. This matches the pattern in the net, so answer option A is correct.

Answer: A

TIMING TIP!

You should always be asking if there are any of the 3R's present when looking at patterns, but it also comes in handy with questions looking at 3D shape nets too.

Example Question 4:

Which of the following cubes can be made from the pattern displayed?

Explanation:

In this question, we have a cube and we are expected to find the net. Here we can pick the butterfly as the reference point; the butterfly is at the top of the cube, so when we look at the nets, we should keep this constant and try to mentally fold the other shapes around it.

Answer Option A: Here the butterfly and duck would be opposite each other if the net was folded into the cube, which is not the correct pattern for the cube in the question. A is, therefore, incorrect.

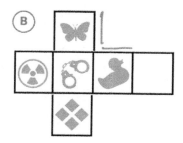

Answer Option B: Again, we have the butterfly at the top, the handcuffs fold next to it and the duck also folds next to it. The two sides lined in purple will oppose each other which matches the cube pattern in the question. Therefore, B is the correct answer.

Answer Option C is incorrect because the duck and handcuffs would fold up opposite to one another, which does not match the pattern in the cube.

Answer Option D is incorrect because the duck is being folded to the left of the butterfly instead of the right, which does not match the pattern in the cube.

Answer: B

Example Question 5:

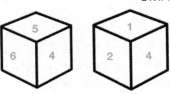

Explanation:

In this question, we are given two views of the same cube, so it's important to find a commonality between the two, to help you understand how it has been rotated. When looking at the cubes, we can see that the commonality is 4, which is in the same position in both cubes. This means the cube hasn't been rotated clockwise or anti-clockwise. The only other rotation we can have is forward or back.

If we assume that it has been rotated forward or back, 5 and 6 have disappeared and have been replaced by 1 and 2, which means 5, 6, 1, and 2 all lie on the same front-back rotation.

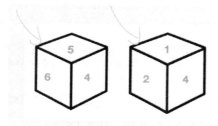

This means that the only side that hasn't changed is the far side that is being pointed to by the yellow arrows. The number that we haven't seen so far is number 3, so this is the number that lies on the far side. It is the digit 4 which will appear on the face opposite to 3, so D is the correct answer.

Answer: D

Expert's Advice!

The position of each side of the cube is important. Think, are there shapes or numbers that can't possibly be next to each other? This will help rule out incorrect answers more quickly.

TAKE HOME POINTS

1. **Answering tricky cube questions.** Using a process of elimination and visualisation is key.

2. **Tackling both 2D and 3D patterns.** Ensure to tailor your approach to the type of cube question presented.

BMAT ONLINE COURSE

 Award-winning BMAT tutorials, designed by our BMAT experts, to guide you through every section of the exam

 Top tips and techniques to construct the perfect answers under time pressure

 Access to past papers, BMAT mocks and question bank to use in your revision

EXCLUSIVE OFFER: GET 10% OFF USING THE CODE BOOK10

Find out more at www.medicmind.co.uk/bmat-online-course/or scan the QR code below

1:1 BMAT TUTORING

 Delivered by current medical students, who have excelled in the BMAT themselves

 Learn how to improve your BMAT technique and speed, to achieve a top decile score

 A personalised 1:1 approach, tailored to your unique needs

EXCLUSIVE OFFER: GET 70% OFF YOUR FIRST LESSON

Book a free consultation today to unlock this offer by visiting www.medicmind.co.uk/bmat-tutoring/or scan the QR code below

CHAPTER 2

BMAT Section II

2.1 BMAT Section 2 Guide

Qualitative preparation for BMAT practice test Section 2

What is BMAT Section 2?

While Section 1 is geared towards assessing more of the generic skills a medical student might have to draw on, BMAT Section 2 puts candidates' scientific understanding to the test.

Once again, it's a multiple-choice assessment (with five to eight options per question). It's only considerably more time-pressurised than the section before it. You'll have 30 minutes in which to answer 27 questions. Exactly seven on each of Biology, Chemistry and Physics, and six on Maths (these numbers used to be less exact).

What do I need to know for BMAT Section 2?

The questions rely on GCSE-level understanding of each of the subjects, which is good news if you're one of many applicants who aren't taking all three sciences at A-Level. Going back in detail through your GCSE (or equivalent) notes should be enough to cover most of the bases.

The only snag is that BMAT Section 2 has its own specification of assumed knowledge. This probably won't match up perfectly to your GCSE syllabuses. Reading it through to spot the gaps in your teaching is a must. If you've continued onto A-Levels, some of them may already have been filled.

The specific topics you need to cover for each section for BMAT Section 2 are covered below:

Biology

- Cells

- Movement across membranes

- Cell division and sex determination

- Inheritance

- DNA

- Gene technologies

- Variation

- Enzymes

- Animal physiology

- Ecosystems

Chemistry

- Atomic structure

- The periodic table

- Chemical reactions and equations

- Quantitative chemistry

- REDOX reactions

- Bonding and structure

- Group chemistry

- Separation techniques

- Acids, bases and salts

- Rates of reactions

- Energetics

- Electrolysis

- Organ chemistry

- Metals

- Kinetic and particle theory
- Chemical tests
- Air and water

Maths

- Units
- Numbers
- Ratios and proportions
- Algebra
- Geometry
- Statistics
- Probability

Physics

- Electricity
- Magnetism
- Mechanics
- Thermal physics
- Matter
- Waves
- Radioactivity

You're also expected to be comfortable with the following SI prefixes that could come up in any of the topics of BMAT Section 2:

Prefix name	Value
Nano-	10^{-9}
Micro-	10^{-6}
Milli-	10^{-3}
Centi-	10^{-2}
Deci-	10^{-1}
Kilo-	10^3
Mega-	10^6
Giga-	10^9

How do I prepare for BMAT Section 2?

Acing the BMAT Section 2

Over fifteen years' worth of past papers are available online, not to mention hundreds of specially prepared practice questions. These will help you get a feel for the style of the questions, the timing of the paper and level of knowledge required. Note that the specification has changed several times in the past, meaning that some questions may no longer be appropriate.

You'll need to spend time revising all four subjects just as if you were taking your GCSEs again. Most of it ought to come back fairly easily! Year on year, though, Physics proves a particular cause of stress for future medics. Remember that only around a quarter of the questions will be on Physics and that the most efficient use of your time is to concentrate on the topics that come up the most frequently – check out our revision guides   to   find   out   what   these   are!

Finally, brush up on your mental and pen-and-paper maths. Unlike in the UCAT, you won't have access to a calculator, so don't bother using one when you take the practice papers. Being able to handle fractions, percentages and sums quickly will pay dividends on exam day.

How is BMAT Section 2 marked?

Just like BMAT Section 1, each question in BMAT Section 2 is worth one mark and there is no negative marking. Your aggregate marks are then converted into a score with 1 being the lowest and 9 being the highest. In our experience, the average BMAT Section 2 score tends to be approximately 5.0 which is roughly 50%. A score of 6.0 or more is brilliant and only 10% of candidates achieve this. Even fewer BMAT candidates tend to get 6.0 (10%) and even fewer get 7.0 Regardless, you can get a few questions wrong and still achieve a perfect 9.0!

What are your top tips for BMAT Section 2?

With 27 questions to be answered in 30 minutes, Section 2 of the BMAT certainly piles on the time pressure. Putting the science to one side, here are ten tips that'll optimise your exam technique and help you make the most of your revision.

1. Lay down time markers

On average, you'll have to complete nine questions every ten minutes. Mentally splitting the section into thirds like this is particularly useful because the response sheet is arranged in three equal columns. Make a written note of the time the section starts and make sure you don't fall behind.

2. Practise under time pressure

Alongside more thorough BMAT revision, trying a few past papers in full under realistic time pressure is an absolute must. It's the best way to turn our timing tips into habit and avoid the horror of not answering all the questions. Remember: you can always go over the practice papers in more   detail   after   you've   finished.

3. Write your workings on the question paper

No extra paper is provided for the BMAT, so when practising, you shouldn't allow yourself any working space beyond the question paper. Get into the habit of writing enough down clearly to continue your train of thought but not so much that you waste time. Full words are a no-no.

4. Use a process of elimination

This one's multi-choice exam technique 101. Crossing out answers that are definitely wrong helps you find the right one more quickly, while also improving your chances of a correct guess if necessary. Questions that ask you to identify combinations of correct or incorrect statements succumb particularly well to this strategy.

5. Fill in your answers straight away

Once you've worked out an answer with reasonable certainty, write it straight into the response sheet. Waiting until the end to do this wastes time since it involves going back through the entire paper. Worse still, you might not get the chance.

6. Don't over-skip

It's advisable to skip the odd question you find hard. But be wary of overdoing this: it throws you off your time markers. Also, it can lead you to panic if you suddenly feel as though you can't tackle any of them. Holding your nerve and concentrating on a question that seems difficult on first inspection will frequently yield the correct answer and boost your confidence.

7. Keep track of skipped questions

Part of the problem with skipping questions is the time wasted finding and refamiliarising yourself with them. Noting down their numbers at the front or back of the exam paper helps you keep track of how many you've skipped and find them with ease.

8. Once you've answered a question, move straight on

Surprisingly, perhaps, many good candidates waste time on questions they've found easy and answered already. When you're under pressure, it feels comforting to work back through such questions and reassure yourself that you've got a handful right with absolute certainty, but you should be focussed on cracking questions you haven't solved yet.

9. Practice your mental maths

In the longer term, sharpening your pen-and-paper and mental maths is a great way to improve your Section 2 scores. Without access to a calculator, you'll have to work comfortably the old-fashioned way with sums, powers, fractions, percentages and decimals – and there's nothing better than BMAT past papers for developing such skills.

10. Bring a watch!

It sounds silly, but don't expect yourself to be within clear eyeshot of a clock on exam day. Sticking to your time markers and knowing when to fill in the blanks with clever guesswork is likely to be pretty hard if you've got no idea how much time you have left.

2.2 BMAT Physics

Guide to BMAT Physics

Introduction to BMAT Physics

We often find that BMAT students stress about the physics element in Section 2. Many BMAT students have not studied physics since GCSE more than a year ago so feel less confident in their ability. If you're in this situation, don't stress! You don't need to revise absolutely everything from GCSE physics and the exam isn't anywhere near as daunting as it first sounds. You might need to do some brushing up, but with some careful practice and preparation you'll find the BMAT physics questions become easier and less daunting.

There will be **6 to 8 questions** testing your physics knowledge within Section 2 of the exam. When you realise how few questions this is in the grand scheme, it doesn't seem anywhere near as bad and is nothing to worry about. Of course, this doesn't mean you can ignore physics entirely as 6-8 marks can go a long way to determine your final score. You should try and maximise your physics ability, but overall don't worry if it's not your strongest subject as you can always make up marks in other areas.

If you find you need some extra help or don't know where to start, we have many handy physics tutorials on our YouTube channel, as well as BMAT courses to walk you through each section.

How do I prepare for Section 2?

The BMAT specification tells you exactly which topics may come up during this section. Remember that the syllabus is at GCSE level, but this doesn't mean the entire GCSE content is needed. In our BMAT course, we go through each specification point, one by one, teaching you the key content you need to remember.

Take a look at the specification and make a note of each topic. You don't want to waste precious preparation time revising for a topic that won't come up! It might be handy to construct a revision timetable and decide which   topics   you're   going   to   study   and   when.

BMAT physics question banks

We've compiled every BMAT past paper from 2009 onwards into a free online question bank. The questions are organised by topic with explained answers. This can help you identify the key topics that come up time and time again, for example in BMAT physics, waves and electricity has been tested 12 times since 2009!

It's also a good way to test your knowledge after you've revised a particular topic. If you've spent a few hours revising waves, it's a good idea to finish your revision with some BMAT questions focused around that topic to test if you're confident enough with the topic to move on.

Which BMAT physics topics should you revise?

It is important to cover the following topics. These are topics that are named in the specification so could be used by the examiners to base questions on. We've counted the number of times each topic has come up in previous exams, so you have an idea of what's the most common. Don't rely on this though! If a topic comes up a lot, this doesn't mean the examiners will definitely write questions on it again this year.

Topic	Number of BMAT Questions (since 2009)
Waves	11
Electricity	10
Energy and Work Done	9
Forces	6
Radioactivity	9
S.I. Units	1
Density	2
Electromagnetism	2
Speed, Distance, Time	3

Topic Breakdown

Within each topic, there are various subtopics that you should familiarise yourself with and be comfortable tackling questions on as listed below:

Waves

- Wave properties

- Wave behaviour

- Optics

- Sound waves

- Electromagnetic spectrum

Electricity

- Electrostatics

- Electric circuits

Magnetism

- Properties of magnets

- Magnetic field due to an electric current

- Motor effect

- Electromagnetic induction

- Transformers

Mechanics

- Kinematics

- Forces

- Force and extension

- Newton's laws
- Mass and weight
- Momentum
- Energy

Thermal Physics

- Conduction
- Convection
- Thermal reduction
- Heat capacity
- Matter

States of matter

- Ideal gases
- State changes
- Density
- Pressure

Radioactivity

- Atomic structure
- Radioactive decay
- Ionising radiation
- Half-life

Top tips for BMAT Physics

1. Don't stress, you may not be studying physics at A-level, but the physics content is aimed at GCSE level, so after brushing up your knowledge it should be manageable.

2. Make a timetable to cover all the topics listed above, ensuring you prioritise the topics that have come up a lot previously in the past, as they're likely to come up again

3. Memorise key formulas and practice using them to ensure you'll be comfortable tackling questions during the BMAT

Final Points

There are additional topics areas covered by the syllabus, but this list gives you a good overview of what topics to brush up on in order to be confident with the BMAT Physics section.

Remember, if physics isn't your strong point, this section also tests biology, chemistry and maths, so there are plenty of places for you to make up marks if you don't perform well in the BMAT physics section.

Finally, if you feel you need a bit of extra help with revising for the Physics section of the BMAT, then why not try a tutoring session with one of our experienced tutors? They are on hand to help you perform best in all aspects of the BMAT.

2.3 BMAT SECTION 2 MOCK 1

1. Which two of the following statements about mitosis are correct?

1. Gene mutations occur mainly in interphase.

2. Allows a variety of species to reproduce by sexual reproduction.

3. Allows damaged and dead cells in a tissue to be repaired and replaced.

4. Four daughter cells are produced, each has the same number of Chromosomes as the parent cells.

A 1 and 2 only

B 1 and 3 only

C 1 and 4 only

D 2 and 3 only

E 2 and 4 only

F 3 and 4 only

2. Carbon is an atom that has 3 isotopes. The mass numbers are 12, 13, and 14. Carbon has an atomic number of 6. Below are statements about carbon and its isotopes.

1. Carbon-13 has 8 neutrons.

2. All of them have the same physical properties.

3. All of the isotopes have 6 protons.

Which statement(s) is/are correct?

A 1 only

B 2 only

C 3 only

D 1 and 2 only

E 1 and 3 only

F 2 and 3 only

G 1, 2 and 3

H none of them

3. The following statements are about Convection.

1. The greater the temperature difference between two objects increases the rate of conduction

2. Colder air is more dense than warmer air.

3. Infrared radiation can travel through a vacuum.

Which statement(s) is/are correct?

A 1 only

B 2 only

C 3 only

D 1 and 2 only

E 1 and 3 only

F 2 and 3 only

G 1, 2 and 3

H none of them

4. The Diagram below shows the cross section of a patio with a square fountain in the middle.

What expression represents the area of the patio?

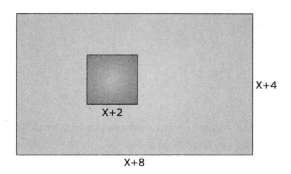

A $4x + 36$

B $8x + 22$

C $2x + 5$

D $8x + 24$

E $5x + 4$

F $7x + 14$

5. Which of the following are correct about stem cells?

1. Once a cell has become specialised, it still has the ability to change into other types of cells

2. Stem cells could be used to treat burns by replacing damaged skin tissue.

3. Pluripotent cells can divide into all types of cells whereas, totipotent cells can only divide into certain types of cells.

A none of them

B 1 only

C 2 only

D 3 only

E 1 and 2 only

F 1 and 3 only

G 2 and 3 only

H 1,2 and 3

6. Nitrogen oxide and carbon monoxide react in a catalytic converter to produce nitrogen and carbon dioxide.

$2NO + 2CO \rightarrow N_2 + 2CO_2$

Which of the following statements is/are correct?

1. Nitrogen oxide acts as an oxidising agent in the above reaction.

2. Nitrogen in N_2 has an oxidation state of 0.

3. Carbon has an oxidation state of -2 in CO_2.

A none of them

B 1 only

C 2 only

D 3 only

E 1 and 2 only

F 1 and 3 only

G 2 and 3 only

H 1,2 and 3

7. The diagram below shows a circuit.

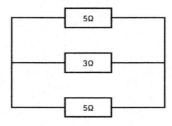

Which of the following statements is/are correct?

1. The total resistance in this circuit is $\frac{15}{11}$ Ω
2. The current is the same at any point in this circuit
3. The total resistance in this circuit is 13 Ω

A none of them

B 1 only

C 2 only

D 3 only

E 1 and 2 only

F 1 and 3 only

G 2 and 3 only

H 1,2 and 3

8. Jack has beaten the world record for the 400m sprint by 10%. Jack takes 90 seconds to complete the 100m sprint. What was the previous world record?

A 95

B 98

C 101

D 100

E 110

F 120

9. Cystic fibrosis is a genetic disorder caused by a recessive allele.

Parent 1 has cystic fibrosis and parent 2 does not have cystic fibrosis. Their child has a child with a person who has cystic fibrosis.

What is the chance of the child having cystic fibrosis?

    A 25%

    B 75%

    C 50%

    D 10%

    E 100%

10. When heated ammonium chloride decomposes into ammonia and hydrogen chloride. The forward reaction is endothermic.

    $NH_4Cl(s) \rightleftharpoons NH_3(g) + HCl(g).$

Which of the following statements about this reaction is correct.

    1. An increase in temperature produces more ammonia

    2. A decrease in pressure shifts the equilibrium to the right

    3. The use of a catalyst will affect the position of the equilibrium

    A none of them

    B 1 only

    C 2 only

    D 3 only

    E 1 and 2 only

    F 1 and 3 only

    G 2 and 3 only

    H 1,2 and 3

11. A block of aluminium has dimensions 10cm by 10cm by 15cm. The block has a mass of 0.75kg. What is the density of the aluminium block?

A 0.65

B 0,5

C 0.6

D 0.8

E 0.75

F 0.9

12. Chris is at the top of a ladder. He can see a ball on the floor at an angle of depression of 30 degrees. The ladder is 5m, how far is the ball from the bottom of the ladder?

A 10m

B 8m

C 6m

D 7m

E 5m

F 8.5m

13. The following table shows some information about respiration and photosynthesis.

Which row is correct?

	Makes ethanol	Produces the most ATP	Makes lactic acid	Is endothermic
A	Aerobic respiration	Anaerobic respiration in animals	Anaerobic respiration in yeast	Photosynthesis

B	Anaerobic respiration in yeast	Aerobic respiration	Anaerobic respiration in animals	Photosynthesis
C	Anaerobic respiration in yeast	Anaerobic respiration in animals	Aerobic respiration	Photosynthesis
D	Photosynthesis	Aerobic respiration	Anaerobic respiration in animals	Anaerobic respiration in yeast
E	Anaerobic respiration in yeast	Photosynthesis	Aerobic respiration	Anaerobic respiration in animals
F	Aerobic respiration	Anaerobic respiration in animals	Photosynthesis	Anaerobic respiration in yeast

Q14. The following diagram shows the electrolysis of aluminium oxide.

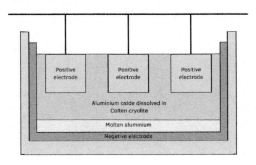

Which of the following statements are correct?

1. The Aluminium ions move to the negative electrode

2. in this process, the positive electrode gets smaller

3. The role of cryolite is to make the electrolysis process quicker.

   A 1 and 2 only

   B 1 and 3 only

   C   1   and   4   only

D 2 and 3 only

E 2 and 4 only

F 3 and 4 only

G 1, 2 and 3 only

Q15. Uranium-238(238-U, 92-U) is an unstable nuclide which is decaying. The emissions during this sequence are either alpha or beta particlesOne of the intermediate nuclides, reached after three alpha and two beta decays, is an element labelled Z.

What is the symbol for this nuclide of Z?

A 234, 86 Z

B 226, 87 Z

C 230, 87 Z

D 226, 86 Z

F 240, 86 Z

F 226, 88 Z

G 230, 88 Z

H 234, 90 Z

Q16. The graphs of the following functions are drawn:

1 $y = 3x-1$

2 $y = x^3$

3 $y = x^2 + 4$

4 $y = 5x + 1$

Which two graphs do not intersect?

A 1 and 2

B 1 and 3

C 1 and 4

D 2 and 3

E 2 and 4

F 3 and 4

Q17. This question is about the digestive system. Which of the following is correct?

1. Peristalsis is the act of excreting undigested material.

2. The role of bile, which is produced in the liver, is to neutralise the acid so that the enzymes in the small intestine have the optimal conditions for digestion.

3. The enzymes required for fibre digestion and absorption are not present in humans.

4. All nutrients can be absorbed by simple diffusion

A 1, 2, 3 and 4

B 1, 2 and 3

C 1, 3 and 4

D 2 and 3

E 1 and 4

F 2 and 4

Q18. Addition polymerisation

What   is   the   correct   structural   formula   of   this   polymer?

$$
\begin{array}{cc}
H & H \\
| & | \\
C & = C \\
| & | \\
CH_3 & Cl
\end{array}
$$

A)

B)

c)

D)

Q19. David puts a 6kg box on a shelf that is 3m from the ground.

A moment later, the box drops and reaches the ground in 5 seconds.

What was the gravitational potential energy before the box dropped and what is the kinetic energy of the box?

Assume that the Earth's gravitational field strength is 10Nkg−1.

	Gravitational Potential Energy /J	Velocity/ms-1
A	240	$\frac{2}{3}$
B	105	$\frac{1}{5}$
C	230	$\frac{1}{8}$
D	170	$\frac{4}{5}$
E	180	$\frac{3}{5}$
F	190	$\frac{1}{3}$

Q20. Points A, B and C are the vertices of a triangle.

A (7, -1), B (2, -8) and C (15, -9). The triangle is reflected in the y- axis and   rotated   180   degrees   clockwise.

Which of the following transformations will return the triangle back to its original position.

A rotation 45 degrees anticlockwise

B translation 3 to the left

C a reflection in the x-axis

D rotation 90 degrees clockwise

E a reflection in the y-axis

Q21. Biomass Calculate the efficiency of the energy transfer below between the secondary consumer and the tertiary consumer?

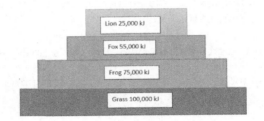

Lion 25,000 kJ

Fox 55,000 kJ

Frog 75,000 kJ

Grass 100,000 kJ

A 73%

B 45%

C 4.5%

D 7.3%

E 75%

F 7.5%

Q22. Bonding

A metal, A, is in group 1 of the periodic table. A non-metal, B is in group 6 of the periodic table. They react together to form a compound.

What is the formula of the compound?

   A A_3B_2

   B AB_2

   C A_2B

   D AB

Q23. A sea ship uses ultrasound to measure the depth of the sea. The speed of the ultrasound in water is 1500 m/s. It takes 3 seconds for the ultrasonic pulse to travel back to the sea ship. Calculate the depth of the sea. (P6.1 Wave properties)

   A 250

   B 4500

   C 500

   D 2250

Q24. A supermarket is selling jars of jam. These are cylindrical in shape. The boxes that are used to carry the jam have a volume of 2700 cm^3. The diagram below shows the dimensions of one jam can.

Height = 5cm

Area of circle = $27 cm^2$

How many jams can fit into 1 box? Assume $\pi = 3$.

    A 25

    B 20

    C 15

    D 14

    E 18

    F 23

Q25. Which of the following types of protein cannot be produced by the genetic engineering of bacteria?

    A hormones

    B Blood clotting factors

    C antibiotics

    D Membrane proteins

    E enzyme

26. Sulphuric acid reacts with iron to produce Iron(III) sulphate.

    $3H_2SO_4 + 2Fe \longrightarrow Fe_2(SO_4)_3 + 3H_2$

(Mr of Iron(III) sulphate = 400, Ar of Iron = 55)

How much iron is required to produce 80 g of Iron(III) sulphate?

    A 36g

    B 26g

    C   22g

D 34g

E 24g

F 27g

27. This question is about Magnetism. Which of the following is correct?

1. To increase the strength of an electromagnet you can reverse the current

2. Iron is a appropriate core for a transformer because its an electrical conductor

3. The generator effect is when a wire carrying a current passes through another magnetic field, creating a force.

4. A permanent magnet's field strength is constant whereas electromagnets field strength can differ.

A 1, 2, 3 and 4

B 1, 2 and 3

C 1, 3 and 4

D 2 and 3

E 1 and 4

F 2 and 4

G 1 only

H 4 only

Answer BMAT Section 2 Mock 1

1. The correct answer is option **B. (B3.1 Mitosis and the cell cycle)**

1 - **True** - This is correct, mutations occur mainly in interphase this is when DNA is replicating.

2 - **False** - Mitosis allows some species to reproduce by asexual reproduction.

3 - **True-** This is one of the main purposes of mitosis, which is to replace damaged cells.

4 - **False-** only two daughter cells are produced and each cell has the same number of chromosomes as the parent cells.

2. The correct answer is option **C. (C1.5 Atomic structure)**

1. **False** –To calculate the number of neutrons, we can use the formula.

   Number of neutrons = mass number – atomic number. Therefore, Carbon-13 has 7 neutrons.

2. **False** - Isotopes do not have the same physical properties because they have different mass numbers. Although isotopes do have the same chemical properties because they have the same electronic configuration.

3. **True** – All isotopes have the same number of protons. Number of

   protons = atomic number.

3. The correct answer is option **G. (P4. Thermal physics)**

1. **True–** Conduction occurs from an object that is at a higher temperature and it moves to an area at a lower temperature. The higher the temperature difference, the faster conduction occurs.

2. **True -** Colder air is more dense than warmer air

3. **True-** Unlike in convection and conduction infrared radiation does not need particles to transfer heat, therefore it can work through a vacuum.

4. The correct answer is option **D. (M4.5 Algebra)**

1. work out the whole rectangular area

$$(x+8)(x+4) = x^2 + 12x + 32$$

2. work out the area of the square fountain

$$(x+2)(x+2) = x^2 + 4x + 4$$

3. Subtract the area of the fountain from the whole rectangular area.

$$x^2 + 12x + 32 - (x^2 + 4x + 4) = 8x + 24$$

5. The correct answer is option **C. (B6.2 Stem cells)**

1. **False** - Once a stem cell has become specialised it cannot change into other types of cells.

2. **True-** Stem cells could be used to treat burns by replacing damaged skin tissue.

3. **False-** Totipotent cells can divide into all types of cells whereas pluripotent cells can divide into some types of cells.

Common trap- Make sure you know your keywords and try not to mix them up.

6. The correct answer is option **E. (C5.1 Oxidation, reduction and redox)**

1. **True-** In Nitrogen oxide, nitrogen has an oxidation state of +2. In the nitrogen molecule, nitrogen has an oxidation state of 0. Therefore, there is a gain of electrons. Use the acronym **OIL RIG**. Oxidation Is Loss (of electrons), Reduction Is Gain (of electrons). Therefore, nitrogen is reduced. Since it is reduced, it acts as an oxidising agent because it oxidises the other species.

2. **True** – Uncombined elements always have an oxidation state of 0.

3. **False** - This is false. Oxygen has an oxidation state of -2. Since there are two oxygen atoms, this gives -4. Therefore, Carbon must be +4 to make the overall charge be 0. Neutral Compounds always have an overall charge of 0.

7. The correct answer is option **B. (P1.2 Electric circuits)**

1. **True** – To calculate resistance in a parallel circuit, the formula below is used.

$$\frac{1}{R} = \frac{1}{R^1} + \frac{1}{R^2} + \frac{1}{R^3}$$

Therefore, $\frac{1}{R} = \left(\frac{1}{5}\right) + \left(\frac{1}{5}\right) + \left(\frac{1}{3}\right) = \left(\frac{11}{15}\right)$

$$R = \frac{15}{11}$$

2. **False** – In a parallel circuit, the current is split into different branches and combines when the branches connect.

3. **False** – This is incorrect, only in series circuit do we add the resistances together to calculate the total resistance.

Common Trap: If you are using the above formula, remember that $\frac{1}{R}$ is not your final answer.

8. The correct answer is option **D. (M2.10 Number)**

This question requires you to have an ability to manipulate between percentages, decimals and fractions.

The new record is 90% of the old record. As a decimal this is 0.90. This is the multiplier.

Use the formula

new = old x multiplier

Rearrange for old = new/multiplier

old = 90/ 0.9 = 100 seconds.

9. The correct answer is option **C. (B4.3 Monohybrid crosses)**

To answer this question, we first need to work out the genotype of the child of parent 1 and 2. Use a punnett square

	a	a
A	Aa	Aa
A	Aa	Aa

We get Aa

Now we draw another punnett square

Aa x aa (since their partner has cystic fibrosis)

	A	a
a	Aa	aa
a	Aa	aa

We get a 50% chance of the child having cystic fibrosis.

10. The correct answer is option **E. (C3.5 Chemical reactions, formulae and equations)**

1. **True** - The Le Chatelier Principle states that when there is a change to a reaction at equilibrium, the position of the equilibrium will shift to the endothermic direction as this will absorb the heat and oppose the change.

2. **True** - A decrease in pressure will shift the position of the equilibrium to the side which has the most moles. There is one mole on the left and two moles on the right. Therefore, the equilibrium shifts to the right.

3. **False** - The use of a catalyst has no effect on the position of the equilibrium because a catalyst increases the rate of the forward and backwards reaction equally.

11. The correct answer is option **B.(P5.4 Density)**

Density = mass/ volume

0.75kg = 750g

To calculate the volume of a cuboid, use the equation= length x width x depth

Volume= 10 x 10 x 15 = 1500cm3

750/ 1500 = 0.5 g/ cm3

12. The correct answer is option **E.(M5.18 Know and use the trigonometric ratio)**

This question requires you to know the trigonometric ratios and you are expected to know the exact trig values for some sin, cos and tan values.

Learn this table below!

	$0°$	$30°$	$45°$	$60°$	$90°$
sin	0	$\frac{1}{2}$	$\frac{1}{\sqrt{2}}$	$\frac{\sqrt{3}}{2}$	1
cos	1	$\frac{\sqrt{3}}{2}$	$\frac{1}{\sqrt{2}}$	$\frac{1}{2}$	0
tan	0	$\frac{1}{\sqrt{3}}$	1	$\sqrt{3}$	–

The first thing we should do is make a labelled diagram with the information

we are told.

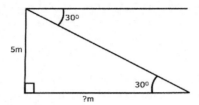

The angle of depression = angle of elevation.

We need to label our hypotenuse, adjacent and opposite so that we can use trigonometry.

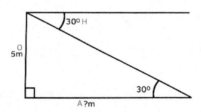

We use
$$\tan\theta = \frac{\text{opposite}}{\text{adjacent}}$$

$$\tan(45) = 5/x \rightarrow x = 5/\tan45$$

x = 5/1 = 5 m

13. The correct answer is option **B. (B9.1 Animal physiology)**

Anaerobic respiration in yeast makes ethanol, whereas anaerobic respiration in animals makes lactic acid. Photosynthesis is endothermic and aerobic respiration produces the most ATP.

14. The correct answer is option **A. (C12. Electrolysis)**

1. **True** - aluminium ions are positive, therefore, they are attracted to the negative electrode

2. **True** - The positive electrode is made from graphite, so it reacts with oxygen and forms carbon dioxide

3. **False** - The role of cryolite is to lower the melting point. This reduces the amount of energy required, so makes the process more profitable.

15. The correct answer is option **F.. (P7.2 Radioactive decay)**

To answer this question, we need to use the two following rules.

1. Alpha decay decreases the mass number by 4 and also decreases the atomic number by 2.

2. Beta decay changes the atomic number by +1(the nucleus gains a proton) and the mass number remains unchanged.

238, 92 U→ (1st alpha) 234, 90 Z → (2nd alpha) 230, 88 Z → (3rd alpha) 226, 86 Z→ (1st beta) 226, 87 Z→ (2nd beta) 226, 88 Z

16. The correct answer is option **B. (M4.12 Algebra)**

The graph $y = 3x - 1$ is a straight line which intersects the y-axis at (0,-1). It has a gradient of 3.

The graph $y = x^3$ is a cubic which passes through the coordinate (0,0) and has a positive cubic so goes from left to right

The graph $y = x^2 + 4$ is a parabola that has a turning point at (0,4)

The graph $y = 5x + 1$ is a straight line which intersects the y-axis at 1

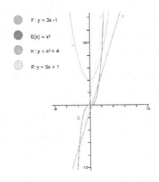

From the diagram above, we can see that $y = 3x - 1$ and $y = x^2 + 4$ do not intercept. This is a common bmat question, so make sure you have more practise!

17. The correct answer is option D. **(B9.2 Organ systems)**

1. **False** - Food moves down the digestive system due to peristalsis. waves of muscular contraction cause this.

2. **True** - This is correct because bile is produced in the liver then stored in the gallbladder. Its purpose is to make sure that when food is going from the stomach (which is acidic) to the small intestines, the enzymes can be in the optimal pH so they do not denature.

3. **True** - The enzymes required for fibre digestion and absorption are not present in humans.

4. **False** - There are multiple ways that the nutrients can be absorbed including simple diffusion, osmosis and active transport.

18. The correct answer is option is D. **(C13.4 Polymers)**

To find out the repeating unit of the polymer, we change the double bond into a single bond. We put it inside square brackets with a small subscript 'n' outside the closing bracket.

19. The correct answer is option E. (P3.7 Energy)

GPE = mgh

6 x 10 x 3 = 180J

S = vt

V = s/t =

V = ⅗

20. The correct answer is option **C. (M5.6 Geometry)**

Firstly the reflection in the y - axis

A (-7, -1), B(-2, -8) and C (-15, -9).

Rotation 180 degrees clockwise. This is because when it is rotated, the x-coordinates and y-coordinates are negated

A (7, 1), B(2, 8) and C (15, 9)

21. The correct solution is **B.(B10.1 Levels of organisation in an ecosystem)**

The first step is to identify which of the animals is the secondary consumer and tertiary consumer. The secondary consumer is the fox and the tertiary consumer is the lion.

The next step is to identify an equation, which is:

Efficiency = (energy available to next level)/ energy from previous level) X 100

=25,000 / 55,000 X 100= 45%

22. The correct answer is option **C. (C6.3 Ionic bonding)**

A metal in group 1 has a charge of 1+, whereas a non-metal in group 6 has a charge of 2-. To balance the charges there needs to be 2 group 1 metal atoms so there can be a 2+ charge to balance the 2-.

23. The correct solution is **D. (P6.1 Wave properties)**

The correct equation to use for this is:

distance= Speed X Time

distance==1500 X 3=4500

This is the distance needed to travel to the sea floor and back so to work out the depth, this value needs to be divided by two.

depth=4500/2=2250m

24. The correct answer is option **B. (M5.15 M5. Geometry)**

We first need to find the radius and use the formula for the area of a circle.

$$\pi r^2 = 27$$

We need to rearrange for the radius.

$$3 \times r^2 = 27$$

$$r^2 = 9, \text{ therefore}$$

$$r = 3\text{cm}$$

Following this we use the equation for the volume of a cylinder

Volume of one cylinder = $\pi r^2 h$

$3 \times 3^2 \times 5 = 135cm2$

Lastly, we divide the volume of the box by the volume of one jar so we can work out how many jams can fit.

$$2700/135 = 20 \text{ jams}$$

25. The correct answer is D, membrane proteins. **(B6.1 Gene technologies)**

Common trap: Make sure you read the assumed knowledge guide and pay attention to small details like this.

26. The correct answer is option **C. (C4.3Quantitative chemistry)**

Mass = Mr x moles

Moles = mass/ Mr = 80 / 400 = 0.2

Moles of iron = 2 x 0.2 = 0.4

Mass = 55 x ⅖ = 22g

27. The correct solution is **H. (P2.2 Magnetic field due to an electric current:)**

1. **False** - To increase the strength of an electromagnet you can increase the number of turns, current and use a softer iron core.

2. **False** - Iron is an appropriate core for a transformer because it can be easily magnetised and also increases the strength of a magnetic field.

3. **False** - The motor effect is when a wire carrying a current passes through another magnetic field, creating a force.

4. **True** -A permanent magnet's field strength is constant whereas electromagnets field strength can differ.

2.4 BMAT SECTION 2 MOCK 2

2019

1. Gene Technology allows us to modify the characteristics of an organism. The following statements are about gene technology.

1. All of the recombinant plasmids will have the desired characteristic

2. The enzyme ligase is used to cut out the gene and the plasmid.

3. Ionic bonds form between the end of the plasmid and target gene.

A   none of them

B 1, 2 and 3

C 1 and 2

D 1 and 3

E 2 and 3

F 1 only

G 2 only

H 3 only

2. Calcium metavanadate contains the following ions: calcium,oxygen and vanadium (V) ,where the vanadium and oxygen form a polyatomic ion with an overall charge of 1- (e.g. CO32-). Which one of the following is a possible formula for Calcium metavanadate?

A CaVO

B CaV_2O_5

C CaVO2

D $Ca(VO_3)_2$

3. The diagram shows a boat with the following forces acting on the boat: upthrust, thrust, air resistance and weight. The boat has a mass of 3 Kg. Which of the following shows the correct horizontal acceleration of the boat?

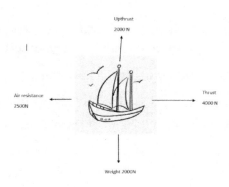

Upthrust
2000 N

Air resistance
2500N

Thrust
4000 N

Weight 2000N

A 4500ms^{-2}

B 500 ms^{-2}

C 1500 ms^{-2}

D 250ms^{-2}

4. Below are two simultaneous equations.

$$p - q = 6 \; ; pq = 9$$

What is the value of p?

A 4

B 7

C 5

D 3

E 6

F 9

5. If two glucose solutions which have varied concentrations are separated by a partially permeable membrane, which one of the following would happen?

1. Once the concentrations of both solutions become equal, active transport would be necessary

2. The solute would move from the more concentrated solution to the least concentrated solution

3. The volume of the more concentrated glucose solution will increase

4. The solute would move from the least concentrated solution to the most concentrated solution

A 1, 2, 3 and 4

B 1, 2 and 3

C 1, 3 and 4

D 2 and 3

E 1 and 3

F 2 and 4

G 1 only

H 4 only

6. An aluminium plate is to be electroplated with silver. Which of the following rows on the table would be suitable for this?

	Anode	Cathode	electrolyte
A	aluminum plate	pure silver	aluminum sulfate
B	pure silver	aluminum plate	silver nitrate
C	pure aluminum	aluminum plate	silver nitrate
D	graphite	pure aluminum	aluminum sulfate
E	aluminum plate	pure silver	silver nitrate
F	pure silver	pure aluminum	silver nitrate

7. A student wants to calculate the density of a stone. They set up an apparatus with a measuring cylinder and water. When the student places the stone in water the volume increases. Calculate the density of the stone.

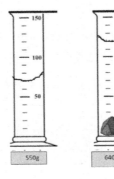

A 1.8 g cm-3

B 0.7 g cm-3

C 1.33 g cm-3

D 0.6 g cm-3

E 2.4 g cm-3

F 1.6 g cm-3

8. Find the value of

$$\sqrt{(4.8 \times 10^6) \div (1.2 \times 10^4)}$$

A 2

B 20

C 400

D 36

E 200

F 40

9. Which of the following does not happen during exercise?1 After exercise, an oxygen debt occurs which is caused by a build-up of lactic acid. This requires an increased breathing rate to overcome

1. After exercise, an oxygen debt occurs which is caused by a build-up of lactic acid. This requires an increased breathing rate to overcome

2. Sweating could occur which causes an increase in the production of the hormone ADH.

3. Glycogen reserves increase as the body takes up glucose

   A 1, 2 and 3

   B 1 and 2

   C 1 and 3

   D 2 and 3

   E 1 only

   F 2 only

   G 3 only

10. Consider the elements in group 7

Which of the following statements are true?

1. This species with the largest Mr reacts the most vigorously with alkali metals to form metal halide salts

2. If potassium iodide solution reacts with bromine water, an orange solution is formed

3. The halogen with smallest atomic radius has the lowest melting and boiling point

4. Atomic radius increases down the group

11. The setup below shows how to spray paint car parts using static electricity. Which of the following is incorrect about the procedure?

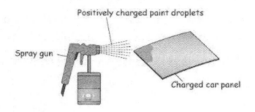

Positively charged paint droplets

Spray gun

Charged car panel

1. The positively charged paint droplets repel each other causing an even spread of paint to the car part.

2. The droplets of paint cannot reach the parts of the car panels that are not in contact with the spray gun as the force of attraction is very weak.

3. The car part is negatively charged which causes an attraction between itself and the positive paint droplets.

A 1, 2 and 3

B 1 and 2

C 1 and 3

D 2 and 3

E 1 only

F 2 only

G 3 only

12. Chris and his wife (2 adults) took their 3 children ice skating and paid £34.50 for the tickets. Maria (1 adult) took her 5 children to the same cinema and paid £36.50.

How much more does an adult ticket cost than a child ticket?

A £2.75

B £1.50

C £3.15

D £4

E £3.50

13. Bees collect nectar from a flower. They use this to produce their food. The bees also transport the pollen from the flower and pollinate other plants so the plants can reproduce.

What type of relationship does the bee and flower have?

A Predator -prey

B Parasitic

C Mutualistic

D Interspecific competition

14. Which of the following are needed for a successful collision?

A A large surface area

B A high temperature above room temperature

C The particles must collide at the correct orientation

D The concentration of particles must be great so there are a lot of particles to collide

15. The following statements are about waves, which statement about waves is correct

A Sonar technology uses radio waves

B Microwave radiation are involved in optic fibre communications

C Gamma ray radiation travels the fastest through a vacuum

D Gamma rays cannot travel through a vacuum.

E A sound wave that has a frequency of 20,000 Hz and a speed of 250 m/s has a wavelength of 80m

16. The pond below has a perimeter of 38m. Find the area.

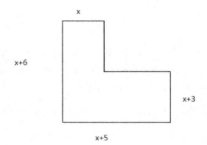

A 72m2

B 84m2

C 68m2

D 76m2

E 96m2

F 92m2

17. In pepper plants, the allele for red fruit colour (R) is dominant to the allele for yellow fruit colour(r). The allele for round fruit (F) is dominant to the allele for long fruit(f)

A pepper plant is homozygous for fruit colour and heterozygous for fruit shape.

Which of the following statements could be true?

1.   The plant has alleles R,r , F, and f
2.   The plant contains R, F and f alleles only
3.   The plant contains r, R and F alleles only
4.   The genotype of the plant for shape is FF
5.   The genotype of this plant for shape is ff
6.   The genotype of this plant for shape is Ff

18. Below is the ionic equation to produce copper hydroxide.

$$Cu^{2+} + 2 NO_3^- + 2Na^+ + 2OH^- \text{---> } Cu(OH)_2 + 2Na^+ + 2NO_3$$

What mass of Cu2+ ions is required to produce 14g of copper (II) hydroxide? (Mr of copper (II) hydroxide = 98, Ar of Copper = 64)

A 9.2

B 8.5

C 7.4

D 9.1

E 8.1

20. **The probability that Sam will be late to school if he was not late the day before is 0.2. The probability that Sam will be late if he was late the day before is 0.4. Sam was not late on Monday, what is the probability of Sam being late on Tuesday and not late on Wednesday?**

A 0.10

B 0.06

C 0.05

D 0.08

E 0.12

21. **The following statements are about DNA.**

1. A nucleotide is made up of a phosphate base and a pentose sugar.

2. A zygote has 23 chromosomes and gets 46 chromosomes when it fully develops.

3. DNA is always found in the nucleus in both eukaryotic and prokaryotic cells.

4. The hydrogen bond that holds the two DNA strands together forms between the phosphate and sugar.

A   none of them

B 1, 2 and 3

C 1 and 2

D 1 and 3

E   2 and 3

F   1 only

G 2 only

H 3 only

22. Thermal cracking can be used to split Dodecane(C12H26). It produces Compound X. Compound X is a hydrocarbon with two double bonds and a relative formula mass of 96. Which of the following compounds is compound X? (C13.1)

A C6H10

B C9H20

C C4H6

D C5H10

E   C8H18

F   C7H12

23. A van of mass 3500 kg was travelling at a speed of 30m/s when it collided with a tree. It takes 200ms for the van to stop.

What is the force exerted on the van by the tree?

A 504 kN
B 525 kN
C 325N
D 464 kN
E 484 kN
F 515 kN

24. ABCD is a parallelogram. AD = <u>b</u> and DC = a. Point Q lies on the line BD, where BQ: QD is 1:4. In terms of a and b, find the vector AQ.

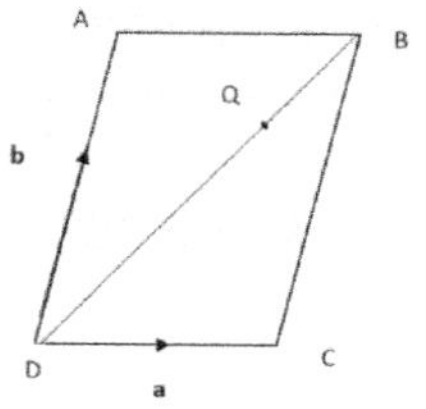

A $\frac{3}{5}$ a - $\frac{1}{5}$ b

B $\frac{4}{5}$ a - $\frac{1}{5}$ b

C $\frac{2}{5}$ a + $\frac{3}{5}$ b

D $\frac{1}{3}$ b

E $\frac{1}{8}$ a + $\frac{3}{4}$ b

25. The thermoregulatory system is a system in the brain that controls the body temperature. On a cold day, which of the following responses can be expected?

1. The skeletal muscles contract quickly and sweating stops.
2. Arterioles constrict to reduce the blood flow near the surface of the skin.
3. Hairs on the surface of the skin stand up to trap an insulating layer of air.
4. Arterioles dilate, to increase the blood flow near the surface of the skin.

A 1, 2, 3 and 4

B 1, 2 and 3

C 1, 3 and 4

D 2 and 3

E 1 and 4

F 2 and 4

G 1 only

H 4 only

26. The atom Chlorine has two isotopes Cl-35 (75%) and Cl-37(25%) . Dichloromethane has the formula CH2Cl2. Therefore the relative masses of dichloromethane will be 84, 86 or 88.

In what relative proportion will molecules of dichloromethane with masses of 84, 86 or 88 occur?

A 9: 3: 1

B 6: 3: 1

C 6: 4: 2

D 4: 2: 1

E 4: 3: 1

F 9: 6: 1

G 3: 2: 1

27. In a lightning system, a transformer is used. Transformer A has 44 000 turns in its 275 kV secondary coil. On the primary coil it has a voltage of 25 kV.

Calculate the number of turns in the primary coil of transformer A and determine what type of transformer this is.

A 2400 and step down transformer

B 1800 and step up transformer

C 2000 and step up transformer

D 2400 and step up transformer

E 1800 and step down transformer

F   2000   and   step   down   transform

Answer BMAT Section 2 Mock 2

1. The correct answer is option A. **(B6.1Genetic engineering)**

False - Not all the plasmids will take up the gene and become recombinant DNA

False - The enzyme ligase is used to join DNA with complementary sticky ends

False - Hydrogen bonds form between the complementary bases in the sticky ends

2. The correct solution is **D. (C5.3 Oxidation, reduction and redox)**

Firstly, using the information that vanadium and oxygen are a polyatomic ion, and have an overall charge of -1, vanadium has a charge of 5+ and oxygen has a charge of 2- . To get to 1+ you need 3 oxygen atoms, which would have a charge of 6- and one vanadium that has a charge of 5+ to get an overall charge of -1 (VO_3-). Next, since calcium is in group 2, it has a charge of 2+. Therefore, you would need 2 molecules of VO_3- to balance the 2+ charge of the Ca^{2+}. So the correct solution is D; $Ca(VO_3)_2$

3. The correct solution is **B. (P3.2 Forces)**

To work out the acceleration, the equation to use is Force= Acceleration X Mass.

The mass has been given, so we need to identify the resultant force horizontally, which is 4000N - 2500N = 1500N. Therefore, the acceleration is 1500/3 = 500 ms^{-2}.

4. The correct answer is option **F. (M4.15 Algebra)**

$$p = 6 + q$$
$$q(6 + q) = 9$$
$$6q + q^2 = 9$$
$$q^2 - 6q + 9 = 0$$

q=3, p = 9

5. The correct solution is **E. (B2.1 Movement across membranes)**

1. True - as the glucose solutions would be in equilibrium and since osmosis is a passive process, active transport would be needed to create a concentration gradient so osmosis can continue.

2. False - because in osmosis the solvent water is moving, not the solutes. Additionally, this is wrong because in osmosis the movement is from a more dilute solution to a higher concentrated solution.

3. True - because water moves from the more dilute solution to the higher concentrated solution, subsequently increasing the volume.

4. False- because in osmosis the solvent water is moving not the solutes.

6. B is correct as the aluminium plate which is to be covered in silver needs to be at cathode. This is to make sure that the silver at the anode can be oxidised and Ag+ ions can be attracted to the aluminium plate.

(C12.6 Electrolysis)

7. The correct answer is **A (P5.4 Density)**

The equation to calculate the density is density=mass/volume. To work out the mass we need to work out the change in mass, which is 640g-550g=90g.

Next, to work out the volume you need to measure the water level from the bottom of the meniscus. So, the change in volume is 120cm3 - 70cm3= 50cm3. Therefore, the density is mass/volume= 90/50 which simplifies to 18/10 when you divide both sides by 5, so the correct answer is 1.8.

8. The correct answer **B. (M2.8 Number)**

Firstly, you divide the numbers on their own without the X10 part. So 4.8/1.2=4.

Next, to work on the powers, since it's a division, you subtract the powers, so 6-4=2. So overall it would be 4X10^2, which simplifies to 400.

Lastly, you square root this which is equal to 20.

9. The correct answer **G. (B9.1 Respiration)**

1 is true as a high breathing rate is used to replenish the low oxygen levels.

2 is true because exercising vigorously can cause sweating which reduces the water content. Therefore, more ADH is released so the kidneys would reabsorb more water.

3 is false. Instead, the body needs to break down glycogen to make glucose so that the glucose can be used in aerobic respiration.

10.

1. False - As you go down group 7 reactivity decreases

2. False - A brown solution is formed because iodine has been displaced.

3. True - fluoride is the smallest one. There are weak intermolecular forces that don't require a lot of energy to overcome

4.   True - Atomic radius increases down the group because there are more shells of electrons

C2. The Periodic Table (IUPAC conventions, Groups are labelled as 1-18)

11. The correct answer is **D. (P1.1 Electrostatics)**

1 is true as like charges repel one another causing an even spread across the car panel.

2 is false because droplets that are not directly passing the panel can be attracted by induction.

3 is false because the car panel is neutral mostly, apart from when the positively charged paint droplets induce a negative charge as they come closer to the panel. The car maintains a neutral charge due to it being earthed.

12. The correct answer is option **E. (M4.15 Simultaneous equations)**

Rewrite using algebra

1a + 5c = 36.50

2a + 3c = 34.50

Double the top

2a + 10c = 73

2a +3c = 34.50

Subtract

7c = 38.5

C = £5.5

Substitute into one of the equations

   A = 36.50 - 5c = £9

The adult ticket is £3.50 more.

13. The correct answer is **C. (B10.1d predation, mutualism and parasitism)**

This is a mutualistic relationship because both the bee and the plant benefit as the bee gets to produce its food and the flower gets to reproduce.

14. The correct answer is **C. (C10.4 Collision Theory)**

For a collision to occur there are 3 criteria. The particles must:

   -collide

   -with energy greater that the activation area

   -when the particles are in the correct orientation

Even though A,B and D can increase the rate of reaction, they are not necessary in collision theory.

15. The correct solution is **E. (P6.1 Wave properties)**

   A. False - sonar technology uses sound waves not radio waves

   B. False - infrared radiation is used in optic fibre communications

   C. False- all EM waves travel at the same speed (speed of light) through a vacuum

   D. False - All EM waves can travel through a vacuum

   E. True - You need to know the formula wave speed(m/s) = frequency(Hz) x wavelength(m), and be comfortable rearranging formulas.

16. The correct answer is option **E. (M4. Algebra)**

Firstly, we must use the information we are given that the perimeter is 38m.

$$X + x+6 + x+5 +x+3 + x+4 = 5x+18 = 38$$

$$5x = 20$$

$$X = 4$$

Next, split the shape and work out the area of each rectangle.

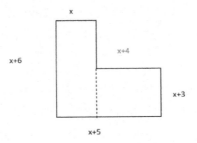

$$x(x+6) \rightarrow 4\ x10 = 40$$

$$(x+4)(x+3) = 8 \times 7 = 56$$

$$40 + 56 = 96$$

17. The correct answer is **2 and 6. (B4. Inheritance)**

1. False - It is homozygous for colour so cannot have both R and r alleles

2. True - This fulfils all the criteria we are given

3. False - It is homozygous for colour so cannot have both R and r alleles

4. False - We are told that it is heterozygous for fruit shape. FF means homozygous

5. False - We are told that it is heterozygous for fruit shape, ff means homozygous

6. True - We are told that the plant is heterozygous for fruit shape so it must have both the F and f allele.

18. The correct answer is option **D. (C4. Quantitative chemistry)**

Moles of copper(II) hydroxide = 14/ 98 = 1/7

Moles of Cu ions = 1/7

Mass = 64 x 1/7 = 9.1

Timing tip: These questions might be best to leave until the end if performing the calculations will take you a long time.

Common Trap: Be really careful with rounding at the end especially because of the timing pressure.

20. The correct answer is option **D. (M7. Probability)**

With probability questions we need to be very careful whether they use the words 'AND' and 'OR'

'AND' means multiplication as they both need to happen

'OR' means addition

The probability for Tuesday = 0.2 and Wednesday is 0.4 as he would have been late on Tuesday. 'AND is used so we multiply.

0.2   x0.4   =   0.08

21. The correct answer is option **A. (B5. DNA)**

1. **False** - A nucleotide is made up of a nitrogenous base, pentose sugar and a phosphate group.

2. **False** - An egg cell and sperm cell both have 23 chromosomes each. When they combine in fertilisation the zygote has the full 46 chromosomes.

3. **False**- Prokaryotic cells do not have a nucleus, they have circular DNA that is not enclosed.

4. **False**- The hydrogen bonds that hold the DNA together form between the nitrogenous bases.

22. The correct answer is option **F. (C13.1c cracking)**

The CnH2n+2 rule can be used to work out the maximum saturation. With every double bond added we take away 2 hydrogens. Therefore, since there are two double bonds, we take away 4 hydrogens. We also need to add up the atoms to get 96. C = 12 and H =1. The only option that fulfils these rules is C7H12.

23. The correct answer is option **B. (P3.6 Momentum)**

To answer this question, we need to know the following equations.

Momentum = mass × velocity

Force = change in momentum ÷ time

Firstly, we are told the mass and velocity so we can calculate momentum.

Momentum = 3500 x 30 = 105000 kgms

Now that we have the momentum, we can calculate the force.

200 ms = 0.2 seconds

Force = 105000 ÷ 0.2 = 525000 N = 525N

Common Trap: *Watch out for units!*

24. The correct answer is option **B. (M5.19 Vectors)**

To be able to answer this question you need to use the vector rule, that in a parallelogram, parallel lines have equal vectors. Therefore, we can also label AB = a and CB = b.

We first need to work out the vector DB. We use the addition law

DB = DA +AB

DB = b + a

To work out AQ we use

AQ = AB + BQ. We do not know what BQ is, however we are told that BQ: QD is 1:4. We can change this into fractions so that BQ =⅕ DB and QD = ⅘ DB

QB= ⅕ (b + a), negate this to get BQ = - ⅕ b - ⅕ a

AQ = a + (- ⅕ b - ⅕ a) =

⅘ a - ⅕ b

25. The correct answer is option **B. (B9.3 Homeostasis)**

1. **True** - Shivering happens because the contractions need energy from respiration. Some of the energy is released as heat so it increases the body temperature.

2. **True** - Vasoconstriction occurs when our body temperature drops below 37 degrees, when the arterioles contract it reduces heat loss from the skin.

3. **True** - When the hairs stand up, it helps to trap in heat to warm up the body.

4. **False** - Vasodilation occurs when the body temperature is too hot, the arterioles widen so that more heat is lost from the surface of the skin.

*Common Trap- It is the arterioles that contract and relax **NOT** the capillaries.*

26. The correct answer is option **A. (C1.5 Atomic Structure)**

For this question it's easiest if we work in fractions.

84 is 35,35 so 0.75 x 0.75 , rewrite as ¾ x ¾ = 9/16

86 is 35,37 so 0.75 x 0.25 , rewrite as ¾ x ¼ = 3/16

88 is 37,37, therefore 0.25 x 0.25, rewrite as ¼ x ¼ = 1/16

Divide all answers by smallest, which is 1/16.

We get

9: 3:1

27.

$$\frac{\text{voltage across primary}}{\text{voltage across secondary}} = \frac{\text{no of turns in primary}}{\text{no of turns in secondary}}$$

$$accept \ \frac{VP}{VS} = \frac{NP}{NS}$$

(P2.5 Transformers)

For physics calculations it makes it easy if we clearly label what information we are provided with.

VP = 25; VS = 275; NS = 22 000

NP = ?

NP = (VP x NS) / VS

25 x 22 000 = 550000 / 275 = 2000

NP = 2000

There are more turns on the secondary coil so this is a **step up transformer.**

CHAPTER **3**

BMAT Section III

3.1 Introduction

Section 3 is the final component of the BMAT. This section of the test differs significantly from the first two with regards to the format. Instead of lots of multiple-choice questions, Section 3 is comprised of just one question - a writing task. The purpose of this final question is to assess written communication skills - which are important for future doctors to have. Doctors are required to make patient notes, write referrals and prescriptions, and sometimes even publish research in scientific journals. Therefore, honing written communication skills will not only improve your Section 3 scores but will also prove invaluable in your future career.

Section 3 Format

Candidates will be presented with three statements and will be required to choose **one** to write a response to. The topics for the statements vary from year to year but typically, there is one **general** statement, one **scientific** statement and one **medical** statement. All statements tend to be philosophical and lay the foundation for further debate. The statements are often given in the form of opinions, quotations and are expressed as if they were factual. The statement will contain three questions for candidates to answer. These questions can be used to structure the response and candidates **must** answer all three questions **comprehensively**. The typical question structure is outlined below.

Statement 'X'

1. Explain what Statement 'X' is referring to.
2. Argue for the statement and/or against the statement.
3. To what extent do you agree with this statement?

Therefore, candidates are Required to

1. Explain what the statement is referring to or the reasoning behind the statement
2. Formulate   an   argument   supporting   the   statement

3. Formulate an argument opposing the statement

4. Reconcile both sides and provide your own opinion on the statement

Common Pitfall!
Typically students who score poorly in Section 3 do not answer all three questions. Candidates MUST answer all three parts of the question to ensure a good score.

Timing

Candidates are given 30 minutes to tackle Section 3. While there is no official word limit for those who are handwriting the exam, there is a space restriction on the answer sheet, which is roughly 3/4th of an A4 page. This typically equates to 300 words but can be between 250 and 350 words depending on the size of your handwriting. For those using a word processor, the world limit is 550 words.

The average person writes at a speed of 20 words per minute, meaning that most people should finish writing their essay in 10-15 minutes. This allows candidates to spend time picking a question, planning the essay and checking over the produced piece at the end. It is important to spend time planning in order to organise your ideas in a fluent and articulate manner.

Overall, the recommended timings are
- 1-2 minutes choosing a question
- 6-8 minutes planning the response
- 10-20 minutes writing the response
- 5 minutes proofreading

These timings demonstrate how planning and writing coherently are key to a successful essay. Quality over quantity is essential in achieving a high score.

Preparing for Section 3

Section 3 preparation is often neglected by candidates as writing practice essays can feel like an overwhelming task. The term "essay" can be daunting, particularly for students that do not take any humanities subjects. If this is something you are struggling with, rest assured that.

Section 3 is not a proper essay - it is only 300 words. Instead of thinking of this task as an 'essay', try thinking of it as a three-paragraph written response. Framing it as three paragraphs and a conclusion can feel a lot more manageable and help students gain motivation to write practice responses.

Expert's Advice!

Taking 30 minutes every week to write a practice Section 3 response can greatly improve written communication skills!

Learning to think, plan and write a high-quality response under timed conditions is difficult so it is important to practice this.

It is important to practice written communication skills consistently through regular practice in the months leading up to the test. Candidates are advised to review their thinking processes once they have completed the essay. This must be done with a focus on highlighting specific weaknesses to work on over the weeks leading up to the test. For example, if you notice that planning is something you struggle with then work on essay planning. Try writing essay plans for all three question options on the practice test or past paper. On the other hand, if you notice that your hand is cramping and preventing you from writing neatly and quickly, try writing out 3/4 of a page of A4 every single day as quickly as possible. You can write anything on the paper, it does not matter - the point is to train your muscles. If you notice that space is a problem and end up running over, get another sheet of paper and rewrite your essay in a condensed format in the allotted space. Over time this will help you identify common trends within your writing where you can be more concise.

Expert's Advice!

Leave your practice essay for a few days, then return to and read it again. This will allow you to be more critical and better identify weaknesses. Utilise your Section 1 skills, trying to draw conclusions and identify the main arguments, and then ensure that these align with the questions.

Analysing your writing after a few days helps prevent unconscious biases in your self-reflections, thus allowing for more thorough feedback.

Candidates who are concerned with coming up with ideas for writing the essay can help widen their knowledge through a range of sources. The type of statement and corresponding questions tend to reoccur over the years, so look at past papers and determine which type of topics are more likely to come up and thus warrant further research. Then use sources such as podcasts, magazines - like The Scientist - and online videos to widen your relevant knowledge.

Expert's Advice!

Make sure to write practice responses to all three genres of statements e.g. medical, general and scientific as appose to just sticking to one format. Many aspiring medics take a natural preference to the medical statement; however, it is important to practice writing responses to the general and scientific statements too. This means that if on the day the medical statement (or your preferred genre) is hard then you will feel confident writing responses to the other statement types.

Common Pitfall!

Some candidates believe that memorising quotes and forcing them into the essay is an effective use of preparation time. Whilst quotes can add value to an essay when used correctly, it is much better to use your preparation time to work on structure and coherence - this is where the marks are.

Take-Home Points

1. Written Communication skills are key. This section assesses this skill therefore honing written communication abilities prior to test day is essential.

2. Approaching Preparation. A positive mindset is necessary for approaching S3 preparation.

3. Timings are key. Stick to the recommended timings to ensure a high-quality,   coherent   response.

3.2 Section 3 Scoring

How is Section 3 Scored?

BMAT essays are scored based on two criteria:

1. Quality of Content - on a scale of 1 (low) to 5 (high)
2. Quality of English - A, C or E

The essays are marked by two examiners and your final score will be one number to represent your quality of content and one letter to represent the quality of your writing linguistics.

Marking Criteria

The boxes below contain information on the marking criteria of the BMAT. Candidates are advised to read through the information thoroughly in order to gain a comprehensive understanding of the expectations required for top marks.

Score 0	An answer judged to be irrelevant, trivial, unintelligible or missing will be given a score of 0
Score 1	An answer that has some bearing on the question but which does not address the question in the way demanded, is incoherent or unfocussed.
Score 2	An answer that addresses most of the components of the question and is arranged in a reasonably logical way. There may be significant elements of confusion in the argument. The candidate may misconstrue certain important aspects of the main proposition or its implication or may provide an unconvincing or weak counter proposition

Score 3	A reasonably well-argued answer that addresses ALL aspects of the question, making reasonable use of the material provided and generating a reasonable counter-proposition or argument. The argument is relatively rational. There may be some weakness in the force of the argument or the coherence of the ideas, or some aspect of the argument may have been overlooked.
Score 4	A good answer with few weaknesses. ALL aspects of the question are addressed, making good use of the material and generating a good counter proposition or argument. The argument is rational. Ideas are expressed and arranged in a coherent way, with a balanced consideration of the proposition and counter proposition.
Score 5	An excellent answer with no significant weaknesses. ALL aspects of the question are addressed, making excellent use of the material and generating an excellent counter proposition or argument. The argument is cogent. Ideas are expressed in a clear and logical way, considering a breadth of relevant points and leading to a compelling synthesis or conclusion.

	Band A	Band C	Band E
Fluency	Fluent	Reasonably fluent/not difficult to read	Hesistant fluency/not easy to follow
Sentence Structure	Good sentence structure	Simple/unambiguous sentence structure	Some flawed sentence structure/paragraphing
Vocabulary	Good use	Fair range and appropriate use	Limited
Grammar	Sound use	Acceptable	Faulty
Spelling and Punctuation	Good with few slips or errors	Reasonable with some slips/errors	Regular errors and frequent slips

Target Score

Setting a target score is a highly personal goal. The graphs below show the 2021 score distributions which indicate that the average candidate obtains a 3.0A in Section 3. As you can see from the criteria above, to score the best possible marks for quality of content, you do not need to have   the   most   knowledge   about   the   topic.

Instead, you need to be able to use the material well and present a coherent argument that is well balanced and compelling. This can be achieved by using a variety of relevant points and covering all aspects of the question. This means that a good essay will necessarily not be one that is creative or original but instead is more likely to be one which is structured well, concise and based on logical reasoning.

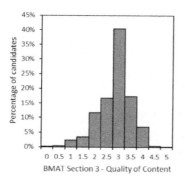 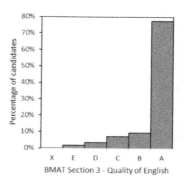

BMAT Section 3 - Quality of Content   BMAT Section 3 - Quality of English

These graphs demonstrate that the majority of students score an A for quality of English. Therefore, it is not hard to obtain an A. Remember to reflect on your own language skills, even if English is your first language, as you may need to improve your grammar and vocabulary to obtain a high letter grade in the BMAT. To obtain an A, candidates simply must not make too many grammar, spelling and punctuation errors. This can be achieved by keeping things simple and using vocabulary that you know.

Expert's Advice!

Having other people mark your practice tests can help identify common errors in your spelling and punctuation. Try swapping with a friend or asking a parent and/or teacher to take a look. Our BMAT team at Medic Mind UK are also happy to lend a hand!

Timing Tip!

Make sure to leave five minutes at the end to check your work for spelling, grammar and punctuation mistakes. These five minutes can make or break your letter grade and so, it is worth being strict about its allotment at the end of your writing time.

What Skills are being Tested?

As stated, Section 3 aims to assess written communication skills. The BMAT specification 2022 states that they are assessing a candidate's capacity to:

- address the question in the way demanded
- organise their thoughts clearly
- express themselves using concise, compelling and correct English
- use their general knowledge and opinions appropriately.

Therefore, producing a logical and coherent response that is concise and well-structured is strongly advised. Similarly, it is important to demonstrate a comprehensive understanding of the question.

Expert's Advice!

How you say it i.e. structure is just as important as what you say i.e. content. Your response must be logical and coherent.

Take-Home Points

1. **Good English Matters.** Make sure to check your work for spelling and punctuation mistakes.

2. **Structure is Key**. Ensure your response is well thought out and follows a logical flow of thought.

3. **Keep it concise.** There are not a lot of words, stick to the key points.

3.3 Choosing a Question

Choosing a question is an important part of Section 3. Candidates do **not** score extra points or credit for choosing a harder question. You are **strongly** advised to choose the question that you feel you could write the most comprehensive, clear and logical response.

Picking a Question

Candidates are advised to spend 1-2 minutes choosing a question. During this time, it is advisable to read through each of the three options carefully. Ensure that whichever question you choose you are able to answer all three sub-questions effectively. When settling on a question ensure you can answer the following questions.

3. Do you have sufficient knowledge to be able to answer the question?
4. Are you able to give examples to illustrate most, if not all your points?
5. Can you address all components of the question?
6. Can you argue for both sides of the argument?
7. Do you find the question interesting? Will you be able to engage in the topic well?
8. Do you understand all parts of the question?

If the answer to all of these questions is yes, then you have likely chosen the best question for you.

Expert's Advice!

Do not pick a question if you cannot present the opposing side of the argument. You must demonstrate that you have considered both sides of the argument or you will not score highly.

Difficulty Picking

It is not uncommon for candidates to struggle to choose a question due to the fact that none of the questions stand out as particularly 'good' or 'easy'. If this happens then it is advisable to take a minute to calm down and do not panic. Instead, ask yourself the six questions above and chose the question that has the most 'yes' responses. Do not begin writing until you have made a clear essay plan based on your knowledge that you know answers all components of the question. This is because you are only given one sheet of paper and so it is not advisable to change questions once you commence writing. Changing question mid-way through writing will waste valuable space on your page and look messy due to crossed out work. Luckily, following the planning advice in this book will prevent this unfortunate event from occurring as you will have a full, comprehensive plan of what to say before you commence writing.

Expert's Advice!

Remember to stay calm in Section 3. Section 2 is very time pressured, so it is natural to feel stressed and time-pressured coming into Section 3. Take a deep breath and try to approach Section 3 in a calm and logical manner.

Take-Home Points

1. **Spend 1-2 minutes picking.** Do not rush into writing.
2. **Ensure you can answer the question well.** Ask yourself the six questions.
3. **Stay Calm.** Take a second to relax and plan your essay well.

3.4 Planning the Essay

Planning an essay well is essential for attaining high marks. The BMAT specification clearly delineates that structure and coherence are critical. Candidates are advised to spend 6-8 minutes planning the essay before commencing writing.

Expert's Advice!

A well-planned essay is a prerequisite for high marks. This is because Section 3 is assessing written communication skills. Clear communication of thoughts requires planning therefore, candidates are less likely to score highly if they miss this step.

How to Plan the Essay

Once you have chosen an essay question, begin by brainstorming all the ideas you have that are relevant to the question. Take a few minutes to write down these points and corresponding examples, then narrow this down to three or four points that will be central to your essay. Once you have decided on these final three or four points, ensure you have a real-life example for each to thoroughly evidence your argument. These points and corresponding examples should form the basis for your essay. There is usually a space on the back page to make notes, it is advisable to use this space for brainstorming and essay planning.

Common Pitfall!
Do not use the A4 page to plan your essay. This space should be reserved exclusively for your written response. The space is valuable and should be treated accordingly. Use the back page for planning instead.

Expert's Advice!

Ensure that you do not just aimlessly jot down numerous points you want to include in your essay. Instead, ensure that you are aware of particular points that you want to focus on, and make sure you are able to easily tell this from your plan when you are writing your essay.

It is recommended to structure the essay around the three sub-questions. When making your plan write out Paragraph 1 and note what you will say in a few words, repeat this for Paragraphs 2 and 3. Below contains a brief outline of a recommended structure, this will be expanded upon in the following chapter.

Experts Advice!

Draw in examples from anywhere, it does not have to be formal readings - it can be from daily life.

Paragraph 1

This can be viewed of as the 'introduction'. In this paragraph, candidates will be responding to the first question. The first question usually takes the format of 'explain the statement [or reasoning behind the statement]' In this paragraph, it is important to really answer the question and contextualise the statement. Candidates should make this paragraph roughly between 50 and 100 words.

Paragraph 2

This paragraph should respond to the second sub-question. Often this will require candidates to argue against the statement. If candidates are asked to present both sides of the argument in the second question, then this can either be done in one large paragraph or split into two paragraphs with one for and one against. Regardless of your chosen formatting, it is essential to present both sides of the argument thoroughly. Presenting just one side of the argument well and one side of the argument weakly will substantially lower your score. Throughout the response to the second sub-question, it is vital weave in strong example to   evidence   your   point.

The response to the second question should be around 150 words.

Common Pitfall!
Be careful not to be biased in presenting the argument. It is vital to balance both sides of the argument in your essay. You can present your own opinion in the conclusion when asked.

Paragraph 3

The final paragraph should respond to sub-question 3 and typically requires candidates to reconcile both sides of the debate outlined above before presenting their own opinion. It is important to tie in everything you have said above in this concluding paragraph and then give your own thoughts on the conclusion. The aim here is not to summarise but to reconcile both sides, instead of just restating your aforementioned points try to consider how they fit together and result in the chosen conclusion. Using words like 'Ultimately' and 'overall' can help signpost that you are about to give your own opinion. The response to sub-question 3 should be between 50-100 words.

Adhering to this structure will help ensure candidates answer all three sub-questions, a pre-requisite for a decent score.

Common Pitfall!

Cambridge Assessment Admissions Testing clearly state that a common trap that candidates fall into is trying to demonstrate their medical expertise instead of sticking coherently to the question. Do not try to force medical facts into an essay. Stick to the relevant examples and focus on ensuring the essay flows.

Source https://youtu.be/aKqKIP0phHs

Expert's Advice!

Be concise! As seen above, the word limit is very short. For example, only 75 words in the introduction. Therefore, it is essential to be concise and get straight to the point.

Take-Home Points

1. **Plan your essay thoroughly**. Make a plan of exactly what you are going to say in each paragraph.
2. **Ensure to answer all the questions.** Structure your paragraphs around the sub-questions to ensure you cover all the key points.
3. **Be concise**. Words are limited so get straight to the point.

3.5 Structuring the Essay

The previous chapter included a brief outline of how to plan the essay. This chapter will delve into the specifics of the essay structure and content in more detail.

Paragraph 1

Often the first question on the statement requires candidates to explain the statement or the reasoning behind the statement. However, often the question statements are very broad and unspecific. For example, the 2020 statements were:

> **1. 'Power tends to corrupt, and absolute power corrupts absolutely.' (John Dalberg-Acton)**
>
> Explain the reasoning behind this statement. Argue that power does not necessarily degrade or weaken the morals of those who hold it. To what extent is it possible for someone to hold power without using it for their own personal gain?

> **2. Science and art once collaborated as equals to further human knowledge about the world. Today, science is far too advanced and specialised to work together with the arts for this purpose.**
>
> Explain what you think is meant by the statement. Argue that science and the arts can still work together to further understanding of the world. To what extent do you agree with the statement?

> **3. There are now many different kinds of internet sites and apps offering medical advice, but they all share one thing in common: they do more harm than good.**

Why might online sources of medical advice be said to 'do more harm than good'? Present a counter-argument. To what extent do you agree with the statement?

(Source: BMAT 2020)

Thus, the BMAT may ask you to explain the statement in the following ways:

- "Explain what you think [statement] means"
- "Explain what this statement means"
- "Explain the argument behind this statement"
- "Explain the reasoning behind this statement."

The BMAT may also ask you to explain the statement in other formats too, for example, Statement 3 in the example above is still requiring candidates to explain the reasoning behind the statement, it is just worded differently. Therefore, knowing how to explain the statement or the reasoning behind the statement is a vital skill for Section 3.

How to Explain the Statement Well

Do

- Explain the statement clearly.
- Contextualise the statement using **relevant** examples - only if they fit.
- Use short and simple sentences that flow logically.
- For Top Scores - Link this paragraph in well with what you are going to say in the rest of the essay.

Do Not

- Misinterpret the quote
- Fail to elaborate sufficiently.

Explaining the statement essentially requires candidates to:

1. Pick out the keywords of the statement. This will be the principle that which the statement is based on. It will be easy to spot what the keywords are as they will stand out from the statement

2. Identify the underlying argument. Use your section one skills to identify the main argument, this is what you will have to explain.

3. Concisely explain this argument. Clearly explain this argument in one or two sentences using the keywords identified.

Expert's Advice!

Top Scoring Candidates often contextualise the statement by bringing in relevant examples. This can be seen in Example Response 1 below that scored 4.0A, this example drew on individuals like Da Vinci and included references to the Renaissance period.

Thus the goal of paragraph 1 is to answer the first question - typically explaining the statement. In order to score top marks, candidates must make their responses coherent. Therefore, it is advisable to set up this paragraph to align with the rest of your essay, a good way to do this is to link your final sentence to what you are going to say in the next paragraph. An example of this can be seen in the exemplar essay below which scored 4.0A, the final sentence of paragraph 1 flows well into the first sentence of paragraph 2.

Additionally, another common feature of essays that score top marks is that in addition to explaining the statement, they also provide a few lines arguing in favour of the statement in the first paragraph. This helps to ensure the essay presents both sides of the argument thoroughly.

Expert's Advice!

You must present a strong case for both sides of the argument. Often paragraph 1 can be a good place to argue in favour of the statement. When explaining the argument, add in relevant examples to evidence to strengthen the case in favour of the statement.

This can be seen in Example Response 1 which scored 4.0A, this essay used the example of art being perceived as a 'hobby' nowadays to strengthen the argument.

Example Essays

Below are some example essays published by the official BMAT examiners. These essays have been marked by the examiners and comments have been attached. All of these essays respond to the 2020 quotes seen above. These example responses and comments are very helpful for candidates to read as they yield immense insight into **what to do** and what **not** to do in the BMAT exam. Students are strongly advised to read through these essays to further their understanding of the ideal format and marking criteria.

Scientific Examples

Example Essay 1

Example essay 1 is an exemplar response to Question 2 that scored 4.0 A.

The first paragraph clearly and thoroughly explains the statements meaning:

> Science and art have always worked hand in hand especially during the renaissance period in Europe. Many great minds (most notably Da Vinci) furthered the human understanding of the universe through the use of paintings, sculptures and statues whilst also increasing human understanding through science. The statement suggests that in the more modern and technologically advanced world we live in today science is far too advanced for art. One might agree with this as art is somewhat of a lost profession. Unlike in the renaissance period, advancements no longer take place in the field with it being seen as more of a hobby or recreational activity whereas science has continued to expand with more technology available to help progress our understanding of the universe.

> Whilst one might agree that art is a lost profession some might say that this doesn't mean that they can't work together.

Science is a very literal and factual field where the goal is to reveal the truth to further human understanding whereas art is about taking your understanding and expressing it in your art. Whilst science is crucial to further human knowledge some might say the more science strays away from art the less human it becomes. The great mystery of the universe turns into a series of numbers. For this reason people might believe that as we are more technologically advanced that now more than ever we will need art to work with science to further human understanding and that it definitely can still work together. To conclude, I can understand what the statement is trying to say with regards to science advancing and art ultimately being left behind. However, to say that they can't work together is wrong and if many people think like this it can be damaging to human understanding. Therefore in the future I hope that art and science can advance together to bring the beauty of human expression and the great mysteriousness of the universe together and then Human knowledge will be at its best.

Source: https://www.admissionstesting.org/Images/630439-past-paper-bmat-2020-section-3-sample-responses-with-examiner-comments.pdf

Examiners Comments:

The candidate has made good use of the material in both parts of the statement: there is a reference to the Renaissance and then a contrast with the present. The candidate has unpacked the prompt material, rather than simply restating it in different words, which is common in less successful essays. (Although the candidate has not capitalised 'Renaissance', this is a minor slip; the language of an essay does not have to be perfect for it to be awarded an A as the language mark.)

The second paragraph has a clear explanation of the difference between science and art, and the candidate provides a reason for thinking that these fields 'can still work together'. One weakness here is the somewhat one-dimensional and rather limited   interpretation   of   science.

The essay is balanced and includes a clear statement of the candidate's view in the final paragraph. Although it was given a 4, it sits towards the bottom of the band because of the superficiality in the counter-argument. The best responses make points as precisely as possible and avoid repetition.

Below an example response to Question 2 that scored 3.0A can be seen which explains the statements meaning.

This statement means that, while the arts once complemented and supported the sciences as much as the sciences supported the arts, this is no longer possible – in effect, scientific disciplines have become too specialised and progressive to overlap with the broader and less revolutionary arts. However, one can argue that this is not the case. As science advances, art is needed as a way to visualise what humans can no longer see themselves. For example, geometric and graphical representations of astronomical events and planets are necessary to turn numerical data into visual forms. Likewise, diagrams and biological drawings are needed for parts of the body doctors and patients cannot regularly observe. As science specialises, there is an equal necessity for the arts. Specific disciplines, for example, turn to the arts for support when they are not helped by other sciences. For example, music therapy and creative activities are implemented in palliative care to help support patients near the end of their lives. There are even whole scientific specialties about the arts such as the study of musical sound waves.

Overall, I disagree with the statement. In the world today, unlike hundreds of years ago, there are many less polymaths – people who work on the arts and sciences in parallel. Although it could be argued that this reveals a lack of collaboration between the two, I believe it rather shows how merged and intrinsic they now are. How could geometrists work without drawing shapes, or surgeons without drawing anatomical diagrams?

So the advancement and specialisation of science has been supported from the very start by the arts, and despite the fact that the arts are not so specialised, in comparison they are still the mortar that hold the bricks of the house of science together.

Source: https://www.admissionstesting.org/Images/630439-past-paper-bmat-2020-section-3-sample-responses-with-examiner-comments.pdf

Examiners Comments:

This essay is a reasonable attempt at answering the question and covers all three parts. Although the candidate offers an explanation of both parts of the statement in the first paragraph, this section of the essay is the weakest: 'complemented and supported' has a similar meaning to 'collaborated' but does not imply that the arts and science were once equals or that they once worked together.

The explanation would be improved by a closer focus on the words used in the question; the most effective essays take a broad view of the terms used in the question and engage fully with the different nuances of meaning

The second paragraph does engage more closely with the statement wording, offering two examples, introduced by 'advances' and 'specialises'. These, however, suggest a somewhat limited understanding of art and the arts. The first highlights the use of art in communicating scientific knowledge. 'Diagrams and biological drawings' do further our understanding of the world, but this is limiting the arts to a technical role. The second refers to music therapy; here, science and arts are working together, but not in a way that furthers our understanding of the world.

The candidate has set out a clear position in the third paragraph, although this is again hampered by a narrow view of art and the arts. The most successful essays set out the strongest possible version of each side of the argument; the candidate's answer here would have been strengthened by working from a broader view of the contribution that art can make.

Below an example response to Question 2 that scored 2.0A. This is a helpful in showing candidates what **not** to do.

Both science and art allowed knowledge about the world to progress through a multitude of ways. Whilst science led to discoveries about the physical world and its inhabitants, art helped to develop the human understanding of emotion and built connections between millions of people.

On one hand, it seems clear that science is too specialised to work with the arts due to its rapid advancement rate compared to art. Science can provide a detailed explanation of most of the things in the universe. It shows what happened in the past and can explain the smallest of details with the use of DNA. In addition, it can predict the possibilities of the future and even estimate major events like the death of the sun and the end of the universe. In contrast, art simply cannot provide this knowledge.

On the other hand, art uses creativity to expand our understanding of the world – something that science may lack. It allows humans to express characteristics/emotions which science cannot. Art can be used to raise questions and curiosity of different aspects of the world. Knowledge can be conveyed between people through the use of art.

In conclusion, whilst science is major in understanding the world, it cannot be solely used as it lacks explanations for things which can only be processed through art. Therefore, I disagree with this statement as both are vital and should be used together.

Examiners Comments

Although this essay makes some reasonable points and attempts to address all three aspects of the question, it treats art and science throughout as separate entities. Since the question focus is on collaboration between art and science and how they can work together, the candidate has therefore (in the phrasing of the marking criteria) 'misconstrued certain important aspects of the main proposition'. The essay has been awarded a 2 as a result.

It is important to engage as closely as possible with the material provided by the question. Discussing the topic area in too general or unfocused a way risks a low mark. Here, the candidate links art to the expression of emotion; while this may be one of the functions of art, the question does not refer to emotion and so the candidate has strayed too far from the topic.

Similarly, it is also important to avoid overly general language in the response. The candidate refers to 'progress through a multitude of ways' (paragraph 1), 'different aspects of the world' (paragraph 3) and 'things which can only be processed through art' (paragraph 4): more precise language here and the inclusion of concrete examples would have improved the arguments.

Expert's Advice!

Reading the examiner's comments gives a clear idea of what is expected. Candidates must give strong arguments on both sides and then clearly state their own opinion.

Medical Examples

Below an example response to Question 3 that scored 3.0A can be seen which explains the statements meaning.

A variety of sites across the internet provide information surrounding medical advice, possible diagnoses and treatments. The regulation surrounding these sites is relatively uncontrolled, leading to many sites providing false information. Only a small proportion give advice which adheres to official guidelines, meaning people may take action which harms instead of helps themselves.

On one hand, with the rise in internet usage, particularly social media sites, medical misinformation is now able to spread much more rapidly. For example, there has been an epidemic of misinformation surrounding Covid-19 vaccinations, which has led to decreased uptake as people only see the misinformation which presents vaccines as dangerous. This may be leading to increased death rates as people lose trust in the medical industry. However, there are also state-endorsed medical sites which can inform people on what to expect from their healthcare. For example, the NHS has a thoroughly reviewed and fact checked website providing accurate information surrounding healthcare. This can allow people to gain more understanding into whether to seek help for their symptoms and how to perform basic first aid. However, the wealth of information may be a threat to the mental health of users as they are overwhelmed and stressed by the options and information.

In conclusion, for the majority of the time, well-regulated sites allow people to have a better understanding of how they can help themselves through first aid or seeking treatment. Despite this, a large proportion of unregulated sites cause people to treat or diagnose themselves incorrectly leading to increased stress or harm. Therefore, I agree with this statement to some extent.

Examiners Comments

This is a reasonably well-argued essay that succinctly engages with all the parts of the question. The first paragraph offers a clear reason why online medical sites might be harmful – because they may provide 'false information'. There are somewhat vague references to 'regulation' and 'official guidelines'; it would have supported the argument to clarify these, if possible. The second paragraph covers similar ground to the first, suggesting that, with the internet, 'medical misinformation is now able to spread much more rapidly'.

The counter-argument – that official sites can help people 'gain more understanding' of 'their symptoms' and 'how to perform basic first aid' – is short but relevant. The final sentence in the paragraph ('the wealth of information may be a threat to the mental health of users') is reasonable, but it logically belongs with the argument that medical websites can cause harm; it is best to group all similar points together, rather than split them across the essay.

The final paragraph provides the candidate's own view and justifies this by reference to the points made above. It is important for candidates to make their own position clear and to justify this. If it is not clear to the examiner what a candidate's position is, the essay will be judged not to have addressed all three parts of the question and the maximum mark it can get will be a 2.

Below is another example response to Question 3 that scored 3.0A can be seen which explains the statements meaning.

Online sources of medical advice is said to 'do more harm than good' because many people on social media platforms offer medical advice for issues they have experienced before. This is likely to not be useful advice as everyone is different and will have varying experiences with medical issues due to the difference in each person's genes. For example, many influencers on platforms like TikTok, YouTube, and Instagram, provide advice about skin care. The followers of these influencers are very likely to buy and use the exact same products, thinking that they will see a huge improvement in their skin texture. However, this is very misleading as everyone has different types of skin, meaning it is not guaranteed that they will achieve good results. This might even result in some of these followers damaging their skin.

On the other hand, the online sources of medical advice may do more good and may benefit many people. Offering good medical advice on the internet is very beneficial for people living in countries where they do not have easy access to healthcare. Online sources provide free and quick medical information for them. There are also many online websites and influencer accounts who are trained in the medical field and offer good medical advice. For example, many dentists have begun to make social media accounts in order to educate more people on how to take care of their teeth and gums, which people of many different age groups find very helpful and informative.

In conclusion, I disagree with the statement because I believe that not all online sources of medical advice do more harm than good. It is only harmful when it is by someone who has no experience at all in the medical field, which is not the case for the majority of popular medical online sources.

Examiners Comments

This is a reasonably well-argued response that clearly covers all three aspects of the question and so has been given a 3. The candidate's response to the statement focuses on social media platforms and provides a reasonable argument, although the example of skincare is not a clear instance of 'medical advice'.

The essay then provides a sound counter-argument, making two good points, first about the benefits of online medical information in countries 'where they do not have easy access to healthcare' and second about social media influencers who have been medically trained. It always strengthens the counter-argument to provide more than one reason in support, as here, or to cover different aspects of the same argument from different angles. In the third paragraph, the candidate clearly states an opinion and provides a reason supporting it.

Below is an example response to Question 3 that scored 2.0A. This is helpful in showing candidates what **not** to do.

Thousands resort to google and apps to diagnose and heal themselves, I am of the opinion this does more harm than good.

Medicine degrees require many years of training and potentially specialisation before one can even become a GP. The average person has not had any of this training and therefore does not possess the necessary skills to spot the important symptoms, know how to correctly describe them, diagnose the illness and most importantly, heal themselves.

Websites and apps get rewarded by clicks and downloads and there is no better way to get these rewards than fear mongering and false promises. This can cause serious harm to the uneducated people trying to treat themselves, as they are none the wiser to the seemingly blatant 'clickbait'. Because apps and websites will prey on the foolishness of the common person, all this can lead to them not seeing their GP or outright harming themselves. I agree with this statement.

Some argue that in light of recent times, where hospitals are critically underfunded, understaffed and underappreciated medical apps and websites can help to relieve pressure. Whilst I believe this point has merit, such as the NHS website or app, other apps out there only cause more harm and result in increased pressure on a healthcare system to not only treat but also to educate. Covid-19 has had a detrimental effect on not only Britain's but all the worlds' healthcare systems, however; websites spreading false information, apps suggesting hopeless treatments in an attempt to grab money and people slowly losing trust for their GP due to google disagreeing, are by no means the solution. To conclude, medical apps do more harm than good as they are a solution to problem yet end up only perpetuating the issue. In the long term there should be more focus on increasing the staff availability in the NHS and other healthcare systems and in the short term, people should be taught to resort to the NHS website for advice, not to some article claiming that injecting yourself with disinfectant or exposure to a 'great light' is the solution to curing a deadly viral infection.

Examiners Comments

The candidate has made a reasonable attempt to engage with the question and states a clear point of view. However, there is no substantive counter-argument and so the essay cannot be given a mark higher than 2.

The first two paragraphs say why 'online sources of medical advice' can 'be said to "do more harm than good"'. The effectiveness of the argument, however, is weakened by the inclusion of obvious background information ('Medicine degrees require many years of training and potentially specialisation before one can even become a GP'): for the BMAT essay, candidates have a limited space to write and it is best to use this space to focus as closely on the argument as possible. There is also some repetitive, dismissive language ('uneducated people', 'the foolishness of the common person'), which does not enhance the argument.

The third paragraph seems to attempt a counter-argument ('medical apps and websites can help to relieve pressure'), but then returns to a discussion of the harm websites can do. The final paragraph, like the second, is weakened by the inclusion of irrelevant information ('there should be more focus on increasing ... staff availability')

Expert's Advice!

Reading the examiner's comments reiterates the fact that candidates must answer all three questions to obtain a high mark. Moreover, all three of these questions must be answered clearly and unambiguously to ensure a score of at least 3.0.

General Examples

Below is an example response to Question 1 that scored 3.0A.

The statement suggests that having power, or opportunity to take advantage of people, leads to the ill use of such power for personal gain, politically, socially, financially, etc, known as corruption. It implies that possession of it is the cause of such action and it occurs without exception, and that the more power, the more corruption. I would suggest this is because it provides opportunity for personal gain, relative to the amount of power, which becomes harder and harder to resist as the power increases.

It is possible Dalberg meant that the very power itself does not cause corruption, but provides temptation and opportunity to those would seek personal gain at the cost of others, and by this logic, those who do not wish this would be well suited to power without taking advantage of it. This idea is echoed widely in our society, as many altruistic groups are providing many opportunities to seek financial gain for example; any charity has money passing to causes, but those responsible could take it for themselves, but don't. Action aid provide money to Covid patients in India, rather than taking it for themselves, as an example of simple altruism.

However, there are a great many examples of where people have had this altruistic opportunity and instead taken it for gain, like the CEO of a successful company paying as little as possible to workers, while taking all they can spare for themselves. There are so many cases of this greed, that it is proof enough that the chance provided by power is so tempting to anyone that it leads to this corruption. And, furthermore, much of the reason that this doesn't occur more is because so many people are vigilant to corruption by those in power – effectively removing the opportunity afforded by the power, re-affirming the idea that when power does not corrupt, it's because the power to be corrupt is not there – as in the case of charities, where books are scrupulously checked and kept, and criminal charges are threatened to those who are corrupt here.

In conclusion, I believe that Dalberg-Acton suggests that power over people, money and resources, provides opportunity for financial gain to those willing to take it, and this becomes more tempting with more power. However, this is not universal and there are examples where people hold power and don't manipulate it – but this is due to genuine altruism, and accountability in many cases.

Examiner's Comments:

The candidate offers a reasonable explanation of the statement, capturing the progressive nature of corruption ('the more power, the more corruption') and suggesting a reason why power corrupts ('this is because it provides opportunity for personal gain'). However, the candidate does not distinguish between 'power' and 'absolute power'. The candidate would need to engage with this aspect of the question to push the essay above the 3 band.

The counter-argument focuses on a single point – altruism – giving ActionAid as an example. This is reasonable but does not discuss whether power can 'degrade or weaken the morals of those who hold it'. As the candidate then returns to the abuse of power in the third paragraph, the opportunity is missed to deepen the counter-argument and strengthen the essay as a whole.

The third part of the question ('To what extent is it possible for someone to hold power without using it for their own personal gain?') is dealt with in the third paragraph, but this simply repeats ideas already covered.

Overall, the essay is a reasonable attempt at the question, but there is a lack of focus on the wording of the statement. Paying close attention to the meanings of the different words in the statement and the question will help generate ideas and improve the focus of the essay. There is 'some weakness' in 'the force of the argument' and 'the coherence of the ideas' (in the phrasing of the marking criteria) but an essay can have these weaknesses, as here, and still merit a 3.

Below is another example response to Question 1 that scored 3.0A.

The statement means that when someone is given power or a position where they can influence others, they will always want more and become greedy. People in power often become selfish and only think about their needs, and in people with absolute power, this happens to a greater extent. An example of this is a dictatorship – their absolute power over a country

corrupts and often they become selfish and try to bend others
to   their   will.

However not all people in a position of power become corrupted. There are many jobs which provide people with power for example a teacher. Teachers have power over their students however they use this to educate and teach inexperienced individuals. Furthermore, members of parliament have strong morals through their promises to the public. When elected and placed in a position of power, their morals don't change. I believe that it is very hard to have power and not use it for your own personal gain.

Our subconscious will always play a role in our decisions and often the decisions made will benefit the person in power. Most often things you believe strongly in affect yourself directly or indirectly so how you use your power will definitely affect you. In history we can see that people in absolute power, for example monarchs and dictators use their power to expand their nation by invading other nations to increase their power and wealth. In conclusion, I believe that people in power use it for their personal gain.

Examiner's comment

The essay provides a straightforward response to the question; it offers a reasonable counter-argument and makes the candidate's position clear.

The first paragraph explains the statement and the candidate recognises the distinction between 'power' and 'absolute power', suggesting a dictatorship as an example of the second. The paragraph could have been improved by closer attention to the wording of the quotation: 'corrupts absolutely' suggests there is a difference between corruption and absolute corruption, which could have usefully been highlighted here.

The counter-argument, in the second paragraph, rests on two examples: teachers and members of parliament. While well-targeted examples can support an argument, examples that are overly general or given without context generally lead to 'weakness in the force of the argument' (in the phrasing of the marking criteria), as is true here.

The candidate would have done better to have thought about why they think teachers and members of parliament do not become corrupted and to have started from that idea.

The third paragraph fully sets out the candidate's own viewpoint and supports this by reference to the subconscious. It is important to make sure that the final part of the question task is fully covered: candidates often do not explain their own view in enough depth, or do not make it clear that this is what they are doing, which can limit the mark they receive.

Common Pitfall!

Cambridge Assessment Admissions Testing body recommends refraining from trying to turn the general question into a medical question. Instead, focus on directly responding to the statement as appose to going off on a medical tangent. It is perfectly acceptable not to include any medicine content in Section 3.

Source https://youtu.be/aKqKIPOphHs

Expert's Advice!

Reading the examiner's comments reiterates that examples must be well explained and directly relevant to the point being made. It is essential that examples fit in naturally to the paragraph and lend credence to the argument being made.

The Second Paragraph

The above examples clearly demonstrate that the second paragraph should respond directly to the second question. Typically, the second question will require candidates to present a counter-argument to the statement. Candidates can be asked to present the counter-argument in a variety of different question formats. For example:

- "Present a counter-argument."
- "Argue that [contrary to statement]"

- "Argue to the contrary that [opposite to statement]"
- "Present an argument to the contrary"

In this paragraph it is important to be clear and coherent, it should be unambiguous that a counter-argument is being presented.

DO

- Clearly Present a counterargument
- Use relevant examples to evidence your point
- Fully Explain the reasoning behind your counter-argument

Do Not

- Try to weaken your counter-argument
- Fail to answer this question comprehensively.

A good way to ensure that the examiner knows that a counter-argument is being presented is to use trigger words at the beginning of the paragraph. For example, beginning the paragraph with:

- On the Contrary,
- On the other hand,
- Conversely,
- Disparately,
- In Contrast,

Common Pitfall!
Sometimes students try to find flaws in their counter-argument or give a weak counter-argument in order to support their overall position in favour of the statement. This is not recommended and can lead to lower marks. The counter-argument should always be strong and comprehensive.

Expert's Advice!

Ensure the reasoning behind your argument is fully explained.

Utilise your Section 1 skills to ensure that your argument flows logically and is based on sound reasoning.

The Final Paragraph

The final paragraph will require candidates to present their own viewpoint **and justify it.** This can be asked in a variety of ways:

- To what extent do you agree with the statement?

- To what extent is it X true?

Question 1 above also demonstrates an example of candidates being asked to present their own viewpoint in different wording.

It is essential that candidates clearly and unambiguously state their opinion. There should not be any doubt over the position when the marker is reading the response. Additionally, candidates must ensure that they have evidenced and justified their position well. Candidates should refrain from just repeating the aforementioned points and summarising what has already been said. The point is to weave everything together coherently and reach a logical conclusion based on this synthesis. This logical conclusion should clearly and unambiguously represent the candidate's opinion. If further examples are needed to strengthen the synthesis and evidence the conclusion it is more than okay to include them in this final paragraph.

Take-Home Points

1. **Structure your essay around the three questions.** Each paragraph should respond directly to one question.

2. **Present both sides of the argument clearly.** The counter-argument should be well explained and properly evidenced.

3. **Weave in relevant examples.** Include relevant examples that are well explained and lend credence to your argument.

3.6 Writing the Essay

Candidates are advised to spend 10-20 minutes writing the essay. If the essay has been well thought out, and planned thoroughly, then this timing is an achievable goal. The essay should be approximately 300 words.

Expert's Advice!

Mark out on your A4 piece of paper roughly where you would like to end each of your paragraphs. This will provide a visual reminder of your approximate word count which will help you to be concise when writing.

Trigger Words

Using trigger words throughout your writing can help with structuring. They are an excellent way to signpost the examiner as to the content of the following sentence. This helps ideas to flow more logically and helps enhance the quality of writing. Below is a list of trigger words that candidates may find useful to familiarise themselves with ahead of test day.

Cause/Effect/Result

- Consequently
- Therefore
- Henceforth
- Accordingly
- Thus
- Hence
- Under those circumstances
- As a result

Agreement

- In addition
- Equally important
- Moreover
- In the light of
- As a matter of fact
- Equally
- By the same logic
- Furthermore
- Similarly

Disagreement

- On the other hand
- Although
- On the contrary
- In spite of
- Nonetheless
- Nevertheless
- Conversely
- Whereas
- In contrast

Examples

- For example
- Especially
- For instance
- To demonstrate
- Namely

- Including
- Specifically
- To illustrate

Emphasis

- Most importantly
- Clearly
- In fact
- Important to realise
- Often overlooked
- In particular
- Above all
- Ultimately

Concluding

- Overall
- In conclusion
- In summary
- Ultimately

Common Pitfall!
Avoid repeating the same words in consecutive sentences. For example, do not begin two sentences in a row with 'furthermore'.

Sentence Structure

Sentence Structure is an important component in the quality of English score. When writing is it important to keep sentences relatively short and concise; as a general rule, sentences should not run over three lines or more. Longer sentences can often confuse examiners and will make your work unclear. If your sentence runs over more than three lines, try splitting it with the use of a semicolon or a full stop.

Expert's Advice!

Don't feel the need to define every scientific term. You may find it useful to define every word however, it will mean that a lot of your word count is taken up, and often the examiner will know what you are referring to. Try to keep everything short and direct

Sticking to the Plan

When writing the essay, it is advisable to stick to the plan as much as possible. This will ensure the response is logical and flows well. Of course, during the writing process you can cross out any points that you feel are no longer necessary; however, be careful not to stray from the plan too drastically. This is because changing course midway through could result in the loss of marks on your Quality of Content as the examiner may be unable to grasp all the points you are trying to get across and your response may lack coherence.

Expert's Advice!

Linking all your points is key! Each paragraph should flow naturally into the next. This is much stronger than making three separate paragraphs with different arguments that are not linked.

Proofing the Essay

At the end, candidates are advised to spend 5 minutes checking over their answers. Proofreading the essay is important to attain an A in Quality of English as small mistakes in the spelling, punctuation or grammar can cost you marks in this area. Similarly, during proofreading try to ensure that the punctuation and sentence structure are somewhat varied in order to ensure the response is interesting. It is important to ensure that you do not repeat a point more than once, as you may lose marks for not being concise. If a point has been repeated numerous times, then cross it out. Finally, the mark of a good essay is being able to read it and deduce what the question was without being told the question. Having this goal in mind can be helpful for highlighting aspects needing further clarity.

Common Pitfall!
A common error is using apostrophes and commas in the wrong places.
Make sure you are comfortable with the correct usage of commas and
apostrophes ahead of test day.

Expert's Advice!

Proofread your essay out loud in your head, this will allow you to
spot errors more clearly.

Take-Home Points

1. **Use Trigger Words.** Trigger Words help signpost the examiner.

2. **Stick to the Plan**. Changing plan mid-course can comprise coherence
in the essay.

3. **Leave time to proofread**. Proofreading at the end will help identify
small errors in spelling, punctuation and grammar for rectification.

3.7 Topic Trends

The BMAT question styles and themes tend to repeat over the years. The following chapter will look at the questions asked over the last couple of years to highlight reoccurring themes in the statements. Although there is no guarantee that these topics will arise again in the coming years, it is worth being familiar with the style of prompts given.

Medical Prompts

- There are now many different kinds of internet sites and apps offering medical advice, but they all share one thing in common: they do more harm than good. (2020)
- Teamwork is more important for surgical innovation than the skills of an individual surgeon. (2019)
- In the age of modern healthcare, every time a patient dies after a routine operation or procedure, it's a case of medical error. (2018)
- The health care profession is wrong to treat ageing as if it were a disease. (2017)
- The option of taking strike action should not be available to doctors as they have a special duty of care to their patients. (2016)
- When treating an individual patient, a physician must also think of the wider society. (2015)

General Prompts:

- Power tends to corrupt, and absolute power corrupts absolutely. (2020)
- People are often motivated to deny the existence of problems if they disagree with the solutions to those problems. (2019)
- Liberty consists in doing what one desires. (2018)
- He who has never learned to obey cannot be a good commander. (2017)

- You can resist an invading army; you cannot resist an idea whose time has come. (2016)

Scientific Prompts:

- Science and art once collaborated as equals to further human knowledge about the world. Today, science is far too advanced and specialised to work together with the arts for this purpose. (2020)
- In science, there are no universal truths, just views of the world that have yet to be shown to be false. (2019)
- Rosalind Franklin said that science gives only a partial explanation of life. (2018)
- The only moral obligation a scientist has is to reveal the truth. (2017)
- Science is not a follower of fashion nor of other social or cultural trends. (2016)

Take-Home Points

1. Reoccurring Themes. Most of the medical prompts take a stance on an ethical issue or debate. The scientific prompts tend to take a stance on the role of the scientist and science in general.

2. Style of Question. All the prompts take a similar style, it is important to be familiar with this format.

3.8 Example Essays

This book has already outlined all the key information and skills necessary to obtain good marks in Section 3. The following chapter will solidify this information by looking at marked example essays produced by the Medic Mind team. These essays are particularly helpful to read through due to the repeating nature of the question style. Thus, these example essays can demonstrate the skills discussed and give candidates inspiration for ideas to write on in the exam.

Expert's Advice!

Reading other people's practice essays, whether a friends or the examples below, will help improve your own essay. Critically assessing other essays will highlight strengths and weaknesses that you can replicate or avoid in your own writing.

Example Essay 1:

Prompt: Doctors should always tell the truth and be honest in their dealings. Explain what is meant by the above statement? Under what circumstances might an honest doctor be justified in being less than perfectly truthful in the course of his or her professional practice? To what extent do you think doctors should always tell the truth?

In essence, the above statement conveys that integrity is one of the most fundamental principles in any doctor-patient relationships. Ethically speaking, doctors should be completely honest in all situations including disclosing a diagnosis to patients that may evoke devastating emotions.

As long as the disclosure is carried out with sensitivity and tactic, doctors should be transparent with patients, regardless of the diagnosis being obesity, terminal stage of cancer or HIV positive. In this way, honestly can facilitate the establishment of trust between patients and doctors which is important to improve patient's well-being. For instance, patients who trust their doctors are more likely to take their professional advice and adhere to treatments. Additionally, patients should also be told about the benefits and risks of a treatment plan as well as possible alternative options. This will allow them to make a well-informed decision regarding their well-being.

However, there are rare yet possible circumstances that permit doctors to withhold truth from the patients. If a doctor is certain that telling the truth will undermine the patient's health, causing irreversible and highly predictable harm, then it is justifiable to not reveal the whole truth to the patient. For example, it would be dangerous to inform a patient of his pancreatic cancer, if the patient is clinically depressed with a high chance of committing suicide after knowing his deteriorating health condition. In this case, not telling the truth may serve in the patient's better interest.

In summary, doctors should always strive to ensure the best interests of the patient. The overwhelming majority of the time this will mean being truthful and honest with the patient however, as stated, there will be the occasional time where not telling the truth may serve the patients best interest. Ultimately, I believe a doctors' integrity is maintained to protect patient safety and to maximise patient's quality of life, if one of the two would be jeopardised as a result of the "truth", it may be wise for doctors to strike a balance between deception and truthfulness.

Examiners Comments:

Excellent Introduction. It perfectly portrays an understanding of the essay question, giving a coherent and well-structured discussion. The paragraph answers the first question well and invokes effective examples to evidence the argument. The second paragraph is very well structured. It answers the second question well, making good use of examples and brings the point across in a concise manner. The conclusion is well composed, taking into account the main question of the essay, and effectively summarising the discussion of the essay as a whole. The student's   opinion   is   well   presented.

This essay would likely score a 4A. English is of a very good quality, and the essay has effectively answered the question without digressing, taking all its aspects into account and coming up with good discussion.

Additional Examples on this Topic

Some additional examples relating to honesty in medical practice are listed below. Students are encouraged to research these ideas further as they may come in use in future essays.

- Duty of Candour
- Medications with better success rates that are not covered by the NHS
- Patient Confidentiality

Example Essay 2:

Prompt: Good surgeons should be encouraged to take on tough cases, not just safe, routine ones. Publishing an individual surgeon's mortality rates may have the opposite effect. Explain what this statement means. Argue to the contrary. To what extent do you think league tables should change a surgeon's behaviour?

Response:

This statement suggests that if mortality rates of doctors are published, surgeons may be deterred from taking more complicated and risky procedures as they are scared it may increase their mortality rates. It suggests surgeons are likely to take simpler cases with a lower risk of mortality that they are confident they can complete successfully. They may do this out of fear of losing their jobs; as they fear a high mortality rate may define their career, which is a risk they may not be willing to take. By publishing mortality rates, people with difficult surgeries may be rejected as the surgeon's won't want to take risky cases, leading to people with more complicated surgeries left without treatment.

Mortality rates should be published as it may lead to surgeons to being more careful while operating as they do not want a high mortality rate, ultimately leading to more people surviving. All surgeons are skilled at their job and therefore should not be threatened by mortality rates, as they   are   likely   to   be   low.

By publishing mortality rates, we can also identify surgeons who should not be practicing if they have an extremely high mortality rate, which can then be looked into and could save future patients who would have otherwise been operated on by a dangerous surgeon.

In my opinion, league tables should not change a surgeon's behaviour. Under the Hippocratic Oath, we have a duty to treat all patients and therefore how complicated the surgery is should not affect the surgeon's behaviour. Also, everyone is aware of the risk of complications within surgery, often ones that cannot be avoided. Different specialties have different levels of risks in their surgery and therefore league tables are of no use and should not change a surgeon's behaviour. Mortality rate is not a reliable factor in the skills of a surgeon, especially in specialties such as neurosurgery where a patient might survive but may be paralysed from their head down. As it is unreliable, no good surgeon should change their behaviour because of published tables.

Examiners Comments:

Good introduction. Clear and answers the question well, and it is clear that the candidate has a good understanding about the topic. This introduction could have been further enhanced by the use of examples and more concise language. Argument to the contrary; answers the question at hand and sticks to the topic while giving a good discussion. Could be better structured and expanded on. Very good conclusion. It answers the question without digressing and manages to combine what is asked as well as personal opinion in a way that leaves the reader leaving satisfied with what they have read. I would give this essay a 3.0A. A mark is lost because the paragraph with the main body could be better structured and expanded upon; however, it still manages to answer the question. The introduction and conclusion have been excellently worked upon. They seem very thorough, and manage to include enough information without getting long-winded or digressing

Example Essay 3:

Prompt: People injured whilst participating in extreme sports should not be treated by a publicly funded health service. Explain the reasoning behind this statement. Suggest an argument against this   statement.

To what extent, if any, does the statement justify a change in public attitudes to personal risk taking? (2010)

The reasoning behind this statement is that participating in extreme sports involves a high level of risk of an extreme injury, as this is their personal choice to accept this risk, they should also accept the risk that if they are injured it will cost the public a large amount of money. This statement argues that the state should not pay for their care, but they should pay for it themselves.

However, there is a grey area surrounding what could be classed as an extreme sport, obvious ones such as skydiving or motor racing have the potential for very serious injuries to occur but what about a sport that is not considered extreme but has the potential to cause extreme injuries. American football has been proven to cause severe brain injuries, but it is not considered extreme similarly with rugby causing serious spinal and brain injuries, should they be treated by a publicly funded service even if they know there is a potential for severe injury?

It could be argued that people participating in extreme sports know that there are risks and so take extra safety precautions first such as safety lines, fire retardant clothing and crash helmets which are not always used in non-extreme sports implying that extreme sports in some ways are safer as they have increased safety measures.

The NHS is an example of a publicly funded health service. When it was set up it was set up to help everyone who needed help; therefore, if a person needs help after partaking in an extreme sport, they should receive that help. Part of the Hippocratic oath is "do no harm" by refusing to treat a patient in a publicly funded hospital and instead insisting they must be moved to a private institution could result in doing more harm through delaying treatment thus violating the oath.

The statement does not justify a change in public attitudes towards personal risk taking as today the public are used to receiving state care that people increase their risk taking every day without thinking about it such as cycling to work, drinking alcohol and walking home and driving in adverse   conditions.

In conclusion the statement cannot be justified as many actions in today's lives increase a person's risk of injury. The statement therefore implies that if you are injured doing anything dangerous you should not be treated by a publicly funded health service. This is not an ethical way to decide who gets treated and who doesn't as many daily tasks could be considered dangerous.

Examiners Comments:

Good introduction. It's concise and to the point, answering the question. The sentences are too long, and this creates errors with the grammar, especially with the use of connectives. Using shorter sentences, or perhaps sentences of varying length, would help to improve the sentence structure and the grammar. Excellent use of examples. There is thorough discussion of the point in question, providing an effective counter-argument. It highlights the problems such a statement poses. This elaboration on the previous point helps build upon the discussion without digressing; this is done very well and helps to provide a stronger counterargument. Another good point in the counterargument, helping to ensure that the discussion takes multiple ideas into consideration. Good answer to the last question. It provides reasoning which links back to the rest of the discussion, and also helps to highlight another point. Could have been improved by further linking the other aspects of the discussion to it and using this paragraph as the conclusion as opposed to having a separate one. The consideration of ethics in this manner is an excellent point to bring up, however, perhaps consider bringing up new points before the conclusion. This conclusion is good and answers the question overall. Perhaps try combine it with the paragraph above. It is very important to know where longer sentences are better, and where shorter sentences are more appropriate. Re-reading the essays done during practice and trying to re-write them so that they sound better when read may help with this and help the sentence structure come more naturally during the final exam.

This would likely score a 4.0C. The content is brilliantly brought out, answering all the questions in a logical and concise manner that make the points of discussion very apparent. To have an excellent essay, the sentence structure and grammar need to be worked on. It seems like the grammatical errors are present as a result of the lengthy sentences making these shorter will help to improve both, creating a much better essay.

Take-Home Points

1. Read Example Essays. This can give you inspiration for content and writing style.

2. Critically Assess other Essays. This can highlight strengths and weaknesses   in   writing.

BMAT ONLINE COURSE

 Award-winning BMAT tutorials, designed by our BMAT experts, to guide you through every section of the exam

 Top tips and techniques to construct the perfect answers under time pressure

 Access to past papers, BMAT mocks and question bank to use in your revision

EXCLUSIVE OFFER: GET 10% OFF USING THE CODE BOOK10

Find out more at www.medicmind.co.uk/bmat-online-course/or scan the QR code below

1:1 BMAT TUTORING

 Delivered by current medical students, who have excelled in the BMAT themselves

 Learn how to improve your BMAT technique and speed, to achieve a top decile score

 A personalised 1:1 approach, tailored to your unique needs

EXCLUSIVE OFFER: GET 70% OFF YOUR FIRST LESSON

Book a free consultation today to unlock this offer by visiting www.medicmind.co.uk/bmat-tutoring/or scan the QR code below

Printed in Great Britain
by Amazon

28407045R00136